HOW TO SEE FAIRIES

DISCOVER YOUR PSYCHIC POWERS
IN SIX WEEKS

How To See Fairies

Discover Your Psychic Powers In Six Weeks

Ramsey Dukes

AEON

First published 2011 by
Aeon Books Ltd
118 Finchley Road
London NW3 5HT

British Library Cataloguing in Publication Data
A C.I.P. is available for this book from the British Library.

ISBN-13: 978-1-90465-837-5

www.aeonbooks.co.uk

I dedicate this book to Pete Carroll, Arcanorium College founder, and to the participants in my course whose enthusiasm and sharing made it such a delightful six-week journey.

Thank you.

Contents

INTRODUCTION

Would you like to be clairvoyant? To have a sixth sense or psychic powers? To read the tarot? To dowse? To see fairies and auras?

If you've started on this book, the chances are that the answer is "yes". Anyone who can already do all these things easily doesn't need this book—though they might find some of the exercises interesting and fun.

It's worth remembering, though, that human culture has been heavily influenced by religious and scientific ideas over many centuries, and that means there are plenty of people who do not want to be clairvoyant—either because they believe it to be something wicked and ungodly, or because they believe it to be a load of rubbish and, if they did start seeing fairies, it would only prove they were mad. In fact, the people who don't want to be clairvoyant are probably a majority (but don't tell my publisher, it might make him sad).

So, let's assume you are not one of those people, and that you really would like to be clairvoyant. That raises the following question: *What makes you think you are not already clairvoyant?*

There are two possible responses. Quite a lot of people have had the occasional weird experience that suggests some sort of psychic ability—a premonition dream, telepathic link or the like. So they get the idea that maybe they have some untapped psychic power, and that thought either scares the shit out of them or else they become curious to find out more—and might buy this book for that reason.

And there are those who find the idea of psychic powers quite fascinating, but have never really experienced anything that could not be explained away. It can range from "I think there's something in it, and would like to see if I can do it myself" to "I don't really believe any of this mumbo jumbo, but who am I to deny it if I've never even tried?"

ISN'T IT ALL A BIT WEIRD?

The idea that there is something weird about clairvoyance and psychic abilities is part of the fascination—it takes us beyond the ordinary and mundane—but it can also be the very thing that *stops* people having those abilities.

Think about it logically—for the unconscious can be quite logical when it is left to act mechanically. You want to be psychic because there is something weird about it; but if you became psychic it would no longer be so weird, in fact it would become part of your everyday experience. For that reason then, you don't really want to be psychic, so you fail to be psychic even when you try to be, and that makes it *really* weird. And that makes you want it all the more...

Another take on this process is: you would like to be psychic because that is something that would set you apart from the common herd, because it is different. If you could be psychic, you would be different. But the common herd has a name for people who are different: they are called "mad". You don't want to be labelled mad, so you don't really want to be psychic even though you think you do and keep trying...

My response to this problem in this book is this: psychic abilities aren't at all weird, they are quite normal. Everyone has them, but many people block them for various reasons, such as the ones I have already suggested. So this book sets out to prove that they are normal by helping you to experience your clairvoyant abilities and to develop those skills.

I apologise for removing the great incentive—the weirdness—but don't worry, because I now offer you something almost as good.

Clairvoyance isn't at all weird, but it can take you to some weird places, should you choose .

Clairvoyance is as natural and normal as walking. Walking can take you to the office—oh how boring—but it can also take you to the scariest mountain top or the wildest scene in town. You can even walk to prison or the insane asylum. It's an ability and it's up to you to use it wisely.

Just in case I've made it all sound a bit too mundane, I invite you now to look at something truly extraordinary.

This amazing picture is a nature deva. Wouldn't it be amazing if we could see and communicate with great beings like this when we walked in nature. What an adventure!

The picture comes from a book called *The Kingdom of the Gods* (1952) by the theosophist Geoffrey Hodson. I came across this book in Bristol public library in my early teens and thought it was terrific—it has many pages of colour plates like this. I later discovered that Hodson's contact with nature spirits began in Sheepscombe Valley, Gloucestershire, about a mile from my childhood home. And now I live in the Cape Province, where he continued his investigations.

HOW I DISCOVERED THAT I WAS NOT PSYCHIC

As a child I wished I could see auras and nature spirits like these—talk about "added value"! I used to sit on Sheepscombe Common and it certainly felt special, and was very beautiful scenery, but I never saw any of the fairies and devas Hodson described. I read the classic books on seeing the aura from our public library and I tried really hard, gazing with half-closed eyes when in a meditative state... etc., etc.

I had no luck with crystal gazing either. I could sort of sense things sometimes—I have plenty of planets in Fire and am supposed to be intuitive—but I was also an intelligent boy having a scientific education and did not want to delude myself. I would not be satisfied with anything less than real clairvoyance, to REALLY see these things.

Later in life I had similar trouble with tarot reading—the symbols are so complex. If I ask for advice on my physics revision and I get a picture like this in the spread, what am I supposed to make of it? "Get on your bike"? How was I supposed to get a REAL reading from the tarot spread and not just wishful thinking?

That was my problem with dowsing too: if I got a friend to hide something in the room and I set out with the pendulum to find it, I'd find myself thinking "I bet he hid it under that cushion" and sure enough the pendulum would then swing in that direction. In other words, the pendulum was simply following my conscious guesswork while I was trying to develop REAL divining skills from my deep unconscious.

So what was all this business about REAL REAL REAL?

Looking back, I'd say that I was blocking my psychic abilities in the manner described above. I very much wanted to gain psychic powers, but I did not want to be crazy. That meant my psychic powers had to be real and provable, not just delusion. So when I began to experience anything psychic, how could I be sure it was not a delusion? Only by testing it thoroughly.

What if I was trying to see fairies and I caught a glimpse of something odd out of the corner of my eye? Rather than just experiencing the oddness from the corner of my eye, I would stare hard at it. Then: "Oh well, I guess it could just have been a leaf moving in the wind..."

Basically my process was this: I want to experience the paranormal. How can I be sure that what I am experiencing really is paranormal? Only by exhaustively testing it to make sure it is not just a trick of the light or whatever. Then how do I know when to stop testing? Only when I have convinced myself it is normal, because if it still seems to be paranormal it might mean that I have not tested it hard enough. So I set out to discover the paranormal, but any glimpse of paranormal activity presented me with a problem that could only be solved by proving to myself that it was not paranormal. (What I have described is one of the basic paradoxes of any scientific investigation of the paranormal.) So I was blocking the paranormal, and I continued to do that until many years later when I began to discover the techniques described in this book.

Over the years I have managed to whittle away much of this resistance to psychic noise, to the point where I can do pretty good tarot readings, use the pendulum regularly, and have even sometimes enjoyed seeing fairies and human auras. It isn't *quite* what I was hoping for as a child, but it certainly adds value to my existence and I believe it could do the same for you.

So this book is about how I did it. A series of simple exercises or practices that you can explore in everyday life to allow your intuition more room to play in. I'm pretty confident that you will be able to see fairies by the time you finish these exercises.

ABOUT THIS BOOK—PREPARATION AND MATERIALS NEEDED

This book is based on a six week online course that I ran during 2008 at Arcanorium College. It consists of an introduction and six weekly sets of course notes with exercises for each week. I have modified the notes for this book and have added sections summarising some of the feedback with my responses and extra thoughts.

When the course requires some materials for the exercise I will explain what is needed, but here are some preliminary notes so you can prepare in advance.

For the fourth lesson it will help if you already have a fully pictorial tarot deck. What does "fully pictorial" mean? Many tarot decks have a combination of cards, some with pictures and some with abstract symbols—typically you have the twenty-two trump cards with pictures, and the court cards (King, Queen, Prince and Princess)—but the remaining cards, like The Six of Wands, just show a pattern of six wands with no people in the picture. What you need for lesson four is a deck where nearly every card has a picture with people in it. The Waite/Rider deck is a common and readily available example. My personal favourite is the Crowley/Harris deck, but it is too abstract and symbolic for the exercises in this book where we require simple people pictures on each card.

Another related project is to start collecting postcards or photographs, also for use in lesson four. Try for a range of at least twenty to thirty images with distinct, strongish themes. By that I mean don't just collect twenty landscape postcards, or twenty pictures of buildings, but go for a real mixture—say a postcard of a cathedral, one of a hillfort, one of a pretty flower, of a car, of a train, a ship, a mountain, an office block, a busy street, a beach, a humorous theme... and so on. By all means include several in the same category as long as they are each distinctive. For example, there is nothing wrong if your collection includes several car pictures, as long as they have very different styles, such as a sports car, a family saloon, an off-roader and a hearse or whatever.

For lesson three you'll need a dowsing

pendulum. I'll explain in the lesson, so this won't be any problem, but by all means look out for a nice one in advance if you feel like it. You might also like to try other divining tools, but in this book I only describe using a pendulum for the sake of simplicity.

You see, this book isn't really about teaching you to dowse, or to read tarot, so much as using those as tools in order to reveal that you really do have clairvoyant abilities so that you can then recognise them and go on to develop and use them in your own way.

Quite a lot of the exercises are best done outside in a garden or in nature, but there is plenty of flexibility, so you need not feel bound by that.

FIRST, A LITTLE BIT ABOUT MAGIC

This course was first presented online at Arcanorium College, a website for people with a general interest in magic and the occult. Although the course did not call for any prior knowledge, I did assume it would be taken by people with some familiarity with magical culture. The same probably applies to most of this book's readers but, just in case, I'll begin with an extra introduction to the magical mindset.

If you don't need this section, by all means move on to the start of the course.

Magic As A Different Culture

I mentioned previously that in recent centuries human society has been heavily influenced by religious and scientific thinking. In fact, it has been dominated by science and religion to the extent that art has been largely subjugated and magic almost driven out.

To illustrate what I mean, consider the way that society accepts religious censure of art—whether it is christians denouncing modern art as pornographic, or moslems attacking literature or cartoons depicting Mohammed. Imagine what would be the response if the situation were reversed and artists demanded that catholic shrines be purged of their "bad taste" kitsch imagery or that the bible needed to be rewritten to iron out the narrative discrepancies between the gospels. The first situation is so familiar as to be taken for granted, but the second sounds outrageous, because art simply doesn't have the authority accorded to religion in our society. On a bigger scale, remember how religious extremism—and the term includes modern "religions" such as Nazism and Communism—assumes the right to lay down rules about what sort of art is acceptable or not.

So much for art—magic has fared far worse. According to religious culture, magic and psychic powers are positively evil or at least ungodly. Although acceptable to more liberal faiths, even practices such as yoga, alternative healing and astrology come under fire from many religious organisations. And in terms of scientific culture magic doesn't even exist except as fraud or self-deception—to claim to be a magician either means you are mad, deluded or a charlatan. Fortunately we live in relative tolerance, otherwise the authorities would have put me either in gaol or a mental asylum for writing this little book.

My "art" example focused on religious domination, but what about science? Surely science has not tried to suppress or dominate art in the same way?

No, not in the same way, but there has been a more subtle tendency for science to belittle art by implying that it is not necessary. The invention of photography could partly be blamed for the crisis in nineteenth and twentieth century painting that lead to the many modern movements and -isms as artists sought to rediscover their purpose.

The most extreme manifestation of this I remember in the 1950s when there were even some scientists suggesting that subjects such as art appreciation and literature could soon be dropped from the university curriculum, because they would become redundant once the parameters of artistic merit had been properly analysed and programmed into a computer. Already in the 1960s "Tin Pan Alley" in London was using computers to generate tunes for potential pop songs, and some thought that was the end for composers.

But what happened instead? A scientist and writer, C.P. Snow, published a speech in which he analysed art and science as "two cultures", suggesting that they represented two different ways of addressing the world, ways that were better seen as running in parallel than in conflict. So science, for all its certainty and wisdom, would never replace art, because art fulfilled a totally different, yet equally real, human need. In this way the potential battle between art and science was defused, and since the 1960s scientists have felt comfortable about enjoying artistic hobbies without feeling obliged to rationalise or explain them in scientific terms.

The funny thing is that religion did not feature in the debate about two cultures. It was only really towards the end of the century—and religious expectations for the millennium—that a conflict began to emerge again, this time between scientific and religious thinking. Although it was not resolved in so many words, it is clear that most thoughtful people came to a similar conclusion: that science and religion were not really at odds, but were two different and parallel cultures serving contrasting and yet real human needs. So that now gave us three cultures: art, science and religion.

What I have been suggesting for many years is that the picture needs to be completed with a fourth culture—magic. Magic also meets real human needs, it is as natural to humanity as religion, art or science, and is best recognised as a culture in its own right. I argued that a lot of things are done by human beings that seem very silly because the denial of magic means that they can only be done in the name of science, art or religion, in whose terms they make no sense—but if they were recognised as magic, they would make perfect sense.

Imagine that some respected sociological research institute came up with a very strong correlation between people who read this book and subsequent marital breakdown. There would be a public outcry for this book to be banned as a danger to society. Even the sociologists would be split between those calling for a ban in face of such incontrovertible scientific evidence, and those insisting that it was unscientific to conclude that this book caused marital breakdown (because maybe people moving towards marital breakdown are those who become more interested in clairvoyance). Both argue that they are being scientific, but in fact those arguing for the ban are not being scientific, they are being magical.

Whereas science argues from causes—so my book must be proven to actually *cause* marital breakdown—magic works from correlations. So if this book and marital breakdown "go together" you could ban this book to reduce marital breakdown—that's called "sympathetic magic". It isn't scientific but it does represent a real human need. If it did not, there would never have been the public outcry for the ban. If this difference between science and magic were recognised, the schism in the scientific community could be resolved by the simple recognition that such threats to society often demand an immediate magical solution, backed by a longer term scientific solution once the real cause had been identified.

PREJUDICES AGAINST MAGIC

You are setting out, with this book, to develop your psychic powers. The psychic powers in question—clairvoyance, tarot reading, seeing fairies, etc.—are all part of the culture I call magic. But, as I suggested earlier, we live in a society dominated by religious and scientific thinking, one in which magic doesn't exist or, if it does, is something very evil.

So you are setting out to experience something that at some level of your being you believe does not exist and cannot be experienced.

You may protest at this and insist "but I do believe in magic", yet I suggest that you don't really, because not even the most experienced magicians really believe in magic. If you don't believe me, then go to some magical get-together and listen to magicians chatting. You'll constantly hear things like "I did this money spell and—it's incredible—the very next day I got a rise at work!" The word "incredible" means *unbelievable,* and it really does in this context because magicians never cease to be amazed that magic works. You wouldn't hear a scientist say "I mixed hydrogen and oxygen and lit it and—it's incredible—it went bang and turned into water" because scientists really believe in science.

That is one of the paradoxes of magic, what makes it so alluring. If something that you really believe in works, it's boring, but if something you don't really believe in works, it's amazing. Nobody really believes in magic, and so we have given it enormous potential to surprise and thrill us.

Follow this course faithfully and I'll blow your mind.

But we do begin with a problem: I am trying to help you to experience something when at some level you believe it is wrong to experience it—either because it doesn't exist, or even because it is evil. To achieve this, the first lesson will focus not so much on reason, or intuition, or feeling, but on the senses.

Reason And Sense

At its best, scientific culture is both reasonable and sensible. But, like any culture, when it has been in power for too long it becomes a line of least resistance for lazy people. In the case of scientific culture, it becomes an excuse to opt for reason and become less sensible, or more detached from reality. To be told that science is not sensible is hard for some who confuse reason and sense, so I'll need to give several examples.

If someone in awe of scientific culture is suffering from backache and I suggest a homeopathic remedy that worked for me, then I can expect a very sceptical response along the lines "that homeopathic nonsense can't possibly have healed you, it's nothing but water." That's a reasonable reply, but it isn't particularly sensible not to try something that others recommend.

If I point that out, I'm likely to be reminded about double blind tests on homeopathic remedies that demonstrated no noticeable healing effect. In other words, people needing healing were given something and did not know (single blind) if it was a remedy or just a dummy pill, and the researchers giving the pill also did not know (double blind). Then it was found that those who actually did get the remedy fared no better than those who got the dummy, therefore it was decided that the remedy was no help.

This is very reasonable, but not at all sensible, because the double blind test has nothing to do with any real-life healing process. How would you feel if you went to the doctor and he said "I'll give you some tablets chosen at random so that I don't know if they are the remedy or not—because I don't want to prejudice your cure with expectations"? Wouldn't that be silly?

Healing involves explaining your illness in a secure environment to an authoritative, sympathetic person who then gives you a remedy that both of you trust—anything less would be cause for complaint. Homeopathic doctors understand this holistic need better than most, so the healing process is halfway there before anything has even been prescribed. It is very sensible, immediate and realistic—it's good magic, unlike woolly objections based on irrelevant tests carried out in some far distant laboratory.

Next, imagine that I become known as someone who always opts for "natural " remedies—herbs, Reiki, meditation or whatever, rather than prescription drugs. Then I get cancer and opt for chemotherapy. My "scientific" critic would find this very funny—"so much for all that natural nonsense, as soon as anything serious happens, he runs straight back to conventional medicine!"

The suggestion is that I am being silly, but truly it is the critic who is being silly. For humans are herd animals with strong social ties, and it makes sense for the survival of such animals to wander forth and explore when there is no danger, but to run back to the herd when there is danger. So it is utterly sensible to explore alternative medicines when faced with minor ailments, and even more sensible to resort to conventional medicine when feeling truly threatened.

I could go on with these examples, but the point is merely to illustrate that the scientific culture has become so familiar that it becomes a line of least resistance for lazy thinkers who rely so much on what is considered to be reasonable that they forget to be sensible. In saying that, I am criticising lazy thinking rather than scientific culture, because in the much rarer circumstance when magical culture has become too familiar, then lazy thinkers begin to rely so much on feeling that they too are just as likely to forget to be sensible.

So my opening exercises will concentrate strongly on the senses. The idea is that we tune up our powers of observation to the point where they are less likely to be influenced by reason. And we do not do that in order to abandon reason, but rather to hold it in check until something has been observed. We no longer refuse to see something simply because "we know it cannot possibly be there".

SOFTENING THE BOUNDARIES BY TUNING THE SENSES

"Hark how the little birds sing of love," sang the old lady on the park bench.

"That's aggression, not love! They're staking a territorial claim when they make that noise," sneered the acne-scarred youth by her side.

Why did he say that? Was the fleeting intellectual triumph really worth the effort? See how quickly the old dear has forgotten his remark and returned to blissful contemplation! But does he look any happier for his knowledge?

They live in two quite different models of reality. Society would call him "strong-minded', but he bears his reality like an irritating burden, whereas she has disciplined the world into a cornucopia of joy. Should we not then admit that, though not so strong in mind, she is at least the stronger in soul?

The above quote comes from a book I wrote called *Thundersqueak* (1979). It reflects a conflict between puritanism and sensitivity.

ARE YOU A PURITAN? OR A GOURMET?

When, for example, I read some glossy magazine article extolling the fine difference between one sort of gourmet delicacy and another, or immensely flowery descriptions of the precise impression that a certain wine leaves on the refined palate, then something in me may protest that so much time and money is being spent on expensive delicacies when there are millions of people on this planet who cannot even afford enough food to stay alive.

For some people, the argument stops there. These are the puritans who would deny all luxury or indulgence for any number of reasons—because the flesh is sinful, because others cannot afford them, because the environment would suffer if we all enjoyed them... or whatever.

Although I can accept the truth of many of these objections, there is a second voice in me that points out that the gastronomic spirit is also a very natural and joyful celebration of existence.

On the one hand I can be angry because the Puritan Spirit in me associates gastronomic refinement with excessive wealth and a desire to show off. On the other hand I know that, once the basic needs of staying alive have been met, even the poorest and most destitute can begin to differentiate between foods that evoke delight and those that simply nourish. Just because one is a homeless tramp does not make it impossible to savour wild berries in Autumn, and I myself can recall just how utterly exquisite was the taste of a simple boiled egg after a week without any food...

In fact the real problem with wealthy food snobs is not so much sensual indulgence as the fact that they can be so obsessed with abstract issues such as the price, the prestige, or the rarity of their indulgence that they fail to tune into its true sensual qualities. They become blunted rather than sensitised by their wealth. Don't we love those tales of wine buffs praising a bottle of cheap plonk onto which some joker has pasted an expensive wine label?

IT ISN'T JUST ABOUT FOOD AND TASTE...

Like the angry young man in the quotation above, there are some people who consistently react against the craze for alternative medicine or organic foods by quoting research showing that it is over-priced, or bogus, or no better for us. On the one hand I know how good it feels to get back at some frightfully smug and dogmatic New Ager by challenging their fads, but on the other hand I know that there can also be a great deal of joy in exploring the options for better food or a healthier life. I am all for joyful exploration and believe that exaggerated criticism of that human need reflects a form of dogmatic puritanism that does not like to see people having too much fun.

WHAT HAS ALL THIS GOT TO DO WITH EXPERIMENTAL CLAIRVOYANCE?

It is all too easy to put the full blame for blocked psychism onto an over-developed intellect, without recognising that there is a puritan tendency that can also form a barrier. The spirit that disapproves of the connoisseur, or the food faddist, or the flaky New Ager, or the twittering "sensitive", is not far removed from the spirit that frowns on any form of magic.

I have some sympathy for people who try not to eat too much microwaved food, but I am irritated when someone refuses to eat *any* microwaved food even when there is no alternative. I am irritated when someone refuses to take some necessary action because of "bad feng shui" or "negative vibrations", and yet I sympathise with those who strive positively to create better feng shui or improve the world's vibrations.

IT'S ABOUT HAVING FUN...

It's the difference between being the victim of one's own sensitivity, and opting for a "sensitivity bonus" to increase the joy of living.

So the first message of this course is that we are seeking to develop our psychic abilities not in order to become enslaved or driven by them, but rather to enjoy the value they can add to our lives.

The second message, then, is what to do about an over-busy intellect that keeps insisting "How can you see fairies when you know they do not exist? When irrefutable scientific evidence for the human aura has never been established?" and so on. This is the voice of reason, a very useful voice when you wish to stop things running out of control, but a real bore when it stops anything at all from happening.

Here again there is a puritan side to reason, when it says "I won't allow this to happen because I know it cannot be real", but there is also a more playful side that can be just as inhibiting. This is the voice that gets so excited when something looks like happening that it rushes in to examine it—rather like the excited child who, having planted a seed, kills it by constantly digging it up to see if it is sprouting. This voice can say : "Wow! I seem to have scored a real hit with that bit of the tarot reading! So I wonder if I'm really psychic, or was it just that I picked up a subtle clue from the punter's body language?" Once you get into that frame of mind you can be so set on finding out "how it works" that you hinder any further results.

THE MAGIC CUP AND THE MAGIC DAGGER

So we need to encourage a different mindset, one that will allow things to develop without slamming on the brakes. To illustrate this mindset

I will use an analogy based on a Cup and a Dagger—two so-called "magical weapons".

The open, receptive attitude that seems to foster clairvoyance is analogous to the Cup, and it is very different from the Dagger of analysis. In the following exercises you will be encouraged to gather sensory data, to explore with all your senses, and I will encourage you to imagine yourself as a Cup, filling up with feeling impressions and simply holding them as a whole, just as a cup holds water.

What you want to discourage at this stage is the tendency in a scientific culture to behave like a Dagger that cuts things open to examine them and analyse into separate parts. For if our Dagger side is over-active, then all impressions get shredded before they can collect.

We are not abandoning the Dagger, simply telling it to wait its turn. First we need to gather impressions in the Cup, and only when we have got some results should we then use the Dagger to see if they were worth collecting.

EXERCISES FOR WEEK 1

The plan is to begin by increasing sensitivity in a way that does not present a direct challenge to reason. We can even catch reason unawares. Nor do we want to challenge the inner puritan that would disapprove of excessive sensitivity.

What would that puritan spirit think if it heard some know-all musical connoisseur say: "I simply refuse to go to that concert because the symphony they are playing should only be listened to lying down"? The reaction might be, "What a load of arty-farty codswallop! How can it matter whether you listen to music lying, sitting or even standing on your head?"

Like the angry young man quotation at the top of the chapter, it's an understandable reaction, but it isn't quite as rational as it might seem. Because, ever since the advent of stereophonic sound, it has become common knowledge that acoustics do vary as you move around in a room, so the position of the listener's head would actually make some small difference. What's more, the experience of music is not directly that of the vibrating atoms of air in the room, but rather how they are interpreted by the human ear and auditory system. Standing, sitting and lying alter the parameters of the balance system governed by the inner ear, and affect other factors like muscular tension and blood pressure.

So the position we are in must have some effect on the musical experience. The only question is whether it is too small to be noticed—can we detect the difference?

EXERCISE 1: LISTENING TO MUSIC

So the idea is to go alone into a room and put on a piece of music fairly loud, then make a conscious attempt to *hear* it more intensely than ever before.

Try to extend your senses so you hear it not just in your ears, but feel the vibrations over your whole body. Give it your total attention—not a narrow analytical attention that separates out the instruments (like the Dagger frame of mind) and analyses the musical score, but rather a complete surrender to the sheer sound in its wholeness (the Cup frame of mind).

Do this for a while, maybe with different pieces of music, until you get a really good feel of listening in a different way, of experiencing the music as never before.

When you have done this to your own satisfaction, then proceed to answer the question: "Does this piece sound better standing, sitting or lying down?" In other words, you know rationally that there must be some difference, so are you able to detect it?

Experiment with that for a while and note your results with different pieces of music for comparison.

The idea is that we are trying to observe something that is very nearly invisible, but with the reassuring conscious knowledge that there really is something to observe. Unlike later clairvoyant experiences, this exercise does not challenge our scientific culture, but simply stretches it a bit to include experiences that it would consider to be trivial, rather than non-existent.

EXERCISE 2: BEING A CONNOISSEUR

Now apply the same approach to explore your other senses. For example, assuming that you are not already a trained wine taster, see if you can make sense of the wonderful descriptions on the back of the bottle. Pour yourself a glass, sit in silent contemplation and sip the wine to see if you can detect the *"sensational alchemy between the sweet flavours of creamy, soft red berries, chocolate covered orange peel and the fragrant, savoury woodiness which, on the palate, wrap themselves around the cool flinty core of this profoundly complex wine"*—or whatever the experts say.

Once again, the inner puritan might want to declare "What a load of rubbish", but remember that the person who came up with this rubbish is probably a highly-trained and paid expert. Again, there must be something in it, but is it something we can tune ourselves to detect?

The sense of smell is a tricky one for many people. You might for example take a selection of perfumes and, instead of asking the simple question "Do I like this perfume?" try something subtler, such as "What sort of occasion would be right for this perfume and what would be wrong?" or "What sort of person should wear this perfume and who should not?"

Sight is difficult for a different reason. Many people are so visual that they have ingrained habits of seeing that are hard to shift. If you take drawing lessons the teacher might well begin with exercises to make you look at things in a new way, seeing them as if for the first time. Rather than try to compete with that, I suggest you move on to the next exercise...

Exercise 3: The Sensual Awareness Meditation

Sit comfortably in an agreeable and not overly intrusive environment and begin by listening to the sounds around you. Do it in the same vivid, fully aware way that you listened to music in the first exercise, but this time you are simply listening to the ambient sound around you. Again, try not to engage the analytic (Dagger) mind that recognises individual sounds and names them, but rather be open (the Cup) to all the sounds together as if they were the totality of a piece of music.

When you have achieved a measure of success at this, move to each of the other four senses, one by one. I suggest vision next: see what is around you in a similar, fully aware way. As before, you do not focus the gaze on individual items so much as become simultaneously aware of the entire 180 degree visual input—being as aware of the peripheral vision as the centre, and not naming what you see. Then try the same with sensation: become aware of the feel of the chair you are sitting on, the breeze on your skin, the position of your body and any tensions or good feelings in it. Smell next, and finally taste.

Note that this is not the same as a "stillness" sort of meditation; the sensing is more active. Although the best approach to sound might be to close the eyes and not move, when it comes to taste you almost certainly need to move your tongue a little to taste what is in your mouth; smell is greatly heightened by increasing the breath and sniffing; to be fully aware of the texture under your fingers, you will do better to move them slightly; and the visual awareness is probably heightened by slight eye movements.

Having run through each sense, you then try to hold that awareness for all five senses at once, to achieve what I'll call total awareness (TA, for shorthand). "Total" is an exaggeration, unless you are highly proficient, because it is very hard to be utterly totally aware. All we require for now is wide open senses and a conscious awareness that is constantly holding those sense impressions and feeling highly aware. Unless you are eating something, the sense of taste will probably get less attention than the other senses, but do at least try to hold sight, sound and body sensation together.

THE QUESTION IS: HOW DO YOU GET ON WITH THIS EXERCISE?

The answer I receive from most people is that, as long as you apply yourself, TA is fairly easy to attain for a few seconds, but hard to maintain.

All too soon you will find your mind has wandered. Either because one sense takes over—as when something interesting is seen and you start watching it and forget the other senses—or else the bored mind starts wandering and you suddenly find yourself daydreaming about something that has nothing to do with your immediate senses.

If that is the case with you, the next exercise should provide a solution.

EXERCISE 4: THE WALKING EXERCISE

Go to some peaceful place—such as the countryside or a quiet suburb—and take a walk, trying to maintain a state of TA as you do so.

Why do I suggest a peaceful place? Not for the value of peace in itself, but simply to avoid the sort of attention-catching distraction mentioned above.

Being in TA, you are vividly aware of everything around you, though trying not to "name" or "think about" any of it, simply receiving and holding the impressions. The Cup not the Dagger.

So, when you inevitably realise that your mind has wandered, and you have lost TA, the fact that you had been in vivid awareness means you can recall your last moments of vivid perception and make yourself turn around, walk back to the place where you had it, and then continue the journey in TA.

Make sure, however, that as you walk back you also maintain TA. So what happens if your attention drifts again before you even get back to where you last lost awareness? You just do the same thing: turn around again, get back into TA, and walk back to the point where it drifted the second time, then continue the journey back to the previous point.

In theory, you might spend the rest of the journey just zigzagging to and fro between two points, each time slipping into a daydream before you have retraced your steps. But in practice I find that the sheer discipline of having to retrace steps does drive the mind to stop its wandering and really hold TA. So with a little practice you will find that you can walk for, say, half an hour and know that most of that time you were in a state of intense, wordless awareness.

The beauty of this exercise is that, because it demands more of you, it is actually much easier than sitting still in a chair and trying to be totally aware. It is a great exercise.

EXERCISE 4: INNER AWARENESS

Answer this question: Do you feel different after such a walk?

What I am asking you to do, firstly, is to practise a sort of inner TA—just turn your senses inward and become aware of your whole inner state. Just hold that state (like a Cup) for as long as you like before answering the question: Do I feel different?

You *will* feel different. In which case, you can, if you wish, go on to explore what is different by being more analytical. What is your bodily sensation, your metal state, do you feel more aware? More peaceful? Or whatever.

This exercise links back to the first one where you looked at your inner response to music heard in different ways—is it different when standing or sitting? Now we ask: are things different when we practise total awareness? What has it left you with?

SUMMARY FOR WEEK ONE

We want to explore our psychic potential. We may have rational resistance to the whole idea of psychic sensing, so we begin by increasing our sensitivity to subtle sensory data at the edge of perception, rather than immediately going full-on for "clairvoyance".

We may also have another form of resistance, a dislike of flaky, fey New Age faddism or a sense that, in a world of so much pain and deprivation, it is sheer bourgeois self-indulgence to want to increase sensitivity, or that discrimination is a dirty word and should be reduced, not enhanced. To overcome that resistance, we focus on the joy of exploration, rather than allowing ourselves to become victims to sensitivity.

So when, in the last experiment, I ask: "What has it left you with?", I am expecting some sort of positive answer. Most people seem to feel good for a while after such an experience. Total awareness adds value to life, and its practice is good for us.

QUESTIONS AND COMMENTS

DOES IT MATTER IF I CAN'T FIND TIME ALONE TO DO THESE EXERCISES?

The first thing I noted in the feedback from these exercises was how readily they could be adapted to suite different daily conditions. I left them simple and flexible because I know that many people are committed to busy work and social schedules, and the exercises could be adjusted to suit these.

For example, it had not occurred to me that the walking exercise might be attempted by a person using a wheelchair, but one of the people on the course did that and their observations were all the more interesting for that:

> This one was personally very difficult but interesting for me. As I use a manual wheelchair, movement in this state is quite strange, particularly given the fact that the situation was overwhelmingly kinaesthetic in nature, almost to the exclusion of other senses. I am usually hyper aware of the contours of the ground I cover, but in practising this exercise I found myself actually paying less attention to my surroundings, and more to the sensations of my body, my hands against wheel rims, muscular movements and tightness, my breath, etc.

One participant was practising awareness in a public place—a courthouse—expanding his listening outwards: "So, I'm sat there, hearing more and more—the inane chatter of lawyers, the mobile phones outside, the grumbling of the central heating..." Then he heard a mumbled conversation about a potential criminal deal, and reported it. "A quick word to a security guard, and crime has been fought for one day, all thanks to [this] excercise!" Not a result I was expecting, but an interesting comment on the possible benefits of awareness.

Another person got an unexpected bonus from the exercise:

> I tried listening to the sounds around me in the kitchen, was impressed at the dishwasher making such a rhythmic nose, when I realized that there was a meeting at the hall down the road to mark a Senegalese festival and it was actual, real drum beats that I could hear. I watched them all reunited nostalgically, grouped together around their drums, keeping up a rhythm that lasted well into the night. I watched one man in a long white tunic walk away with such a joyful spring to his step that it made me laugh.

This is another example of how one can set out to expand one's universe a little by learning a new skill, and find little side-benefits from the exercises adding extra value to life—a conversation overheard, a discovery of an interesting spectacle down the street that one might never have witnessed in normal consciousness.

Although I specify a particular way of doing these exercises for the sake of clarity, they are in fact very adaptable to everyday life once you get the basic principle. It is a way of listening—rather than a way of listening just to music.

THIS TOTAL AWARENESS, AM I MEANT TO GO INTO A SORT OF TRANCE?

If by "trance" you mean a turning inward, or you mean a narrowing down of the attention for economy of effort—like the times when you are so focused on driving that you are not aware of anything other than the road—then what we are exploring would seem quite the opposite of trance. And yet what we are doing can shift consciousness in the same way that a trance does.

If, instead of opening up his hearing to everything around, the writer above had been a security guard specifically listening out for signs of crime, would he have been more, or less likely to hear that conversation? It is an interesting question.

But I suggest that for most of our evolutionary history we would have had our senses wide open for all impressions. When walking in the wild, danger can take so many forms—a lion's footprint or the trembling of a branch, the hiss of a snake or buzz of a mosquito, a smell of rhino shit or of fire, and so on. This was confirmed by one of the participants who had been taught a similar exercise as part of the Kamana Program of the Wilderness Awareness School, described as "a mix of native wisdom and field biology". He mentioned an interesting extension of the awareness exercise that you could experiment with:

> One of the things they taught was to imagine each sense being a different animal: Owl for

sight, Deer for hearing, Raccoon for touch, Dog for smell, Fox or Cat for movement. One then pulled it all together and became the Wolf. For me this helps.

So I reckon that human beings, like most animals, evolved to be hard-wired for wide open senses, and that modern living has narrowed down the threats so that we have gained a greater ability to concentrate, but that we do not practise open awareness sufficiently. That could explain why it feels so good when you do practise it. As one participant wrote:

> Things seemed more beautiful and more weird—hearing sounds without taking for granted where they were coming from made listening a much more interesting experience... It had the effect of making me feel liberated, I suppose from emotions and attachment. Everything seemed new, it was a bit like being on holiday or waking up first thing in the morning, before you remember all the stuff you've got to do.

Another wrote:

> I did find that focusing on the environment as fully as possible took the focus away from all the stuff going on in my head, leading to a meditative state. Even if I did struggle with maintaining TA, at least I learnt a way of clearing my mind and reducing anxiety that can be used in daily situations.

IF I CAN'T MANAGE THE WALKING EXERCISE, IS THE SEATED ONE OKAY?

Exercise 4, the walking awareness exercise, makes it much easier to get results because of the physical discipline involved in making yourself walk back every time to the point where awareness was lost. It is the better exercise.

The reason I suggested you start with Exercise 3—the seated sensory awareness—was to get you used to the idea, and to find how difficult it is to maintain high awareness and not fall into daydreams when simply sitting still. So it was good preparation for the more effective Exercise 4.

There is one problem that did not occur to me when I first taught this course. In some locations there is no place where it is safe for someone to walk alone in nature, especially not a woman on her own. Even if that is just ninety-nine percent paranoia, it is hard to get into the exercise if you do not feel safe. Thinking it over, I have one possible solution that might work—do the exercise in a museum, art gallery, stately home or similar visitor attraction.

There are likely to be people around, but that is the sort of environment where you can meander dreamily without attracting attention, and where other people have better things to stare at than yourself. The other key point is that it is an environment that presents a string of new unfamiliar sights—unlike a too-familiar home environment. This means it is easier to remember and go back to the last thing you noticed before drifting off.

Are All The Senses Equally Important?

Some people had difficulty with particular senses. Smell and taste can be difficult when seated indoors, because they are relatively static. When walking there is a greater variety of smells and you notice the changes. Two things I've tried in the past have been to hold a herb leaf in my mouth slowly releasing its flavour (certainly more stimulating, but it can drown out more subtle tastes) or else slightly opening the mouth and tasting the air, which can reinforce the smell sensation sometimes. One writer was fine with smells when seated out of doors:

> I now became distinctly aware of the scents of those passing me, the whiffs of perfumes and body-sprays, and my tongue felt heavy in my mouth as I became aware, again, of that rising sense of joy and excitement I mentioned in the previous exercise. As it rose, it seemed to pull me out of the space I had occupied, into normal consciousness.

At the other extreme, one person was so sensitive to hearing that it tended to dominate other senses, but he found a novel solution: "After putting on some earplugs, I could extend this awareness much longer!" Another found: "It was useful to listen to the sound as cadences and rhythms rather than particulate, individual sounds. This may be because I grew up by the sea and used to spend time meditating to the sound of the waves."

Another was having problems with interference between the senses, and with thinking too much:

> I was trying to get in a TA state, and when I was catching myself thinking of something I turned back to the place I estimated I had started thinking, so I had to go back quite a few times. Although sometimes I felt embarrassed in front of a couple of passers-by who were scratching their heads, trying to figure out what I was doing, I persisted. I noticed that most of the time I was catching myself thinking that I shouldn't think. Quite a vicious circle. Maybe if I was concentrating on something, like my breathing, that would make the whole experience easier. I don't know. The end result was that I've made a forty-minute walk three times longer.

I HAVE TROUBLE CONCENTRATING ON ONE SENSE

The person quoted above tended to write about "concentrating" on one or other senses, so I suggested he should instead think of "opening up" a sense. I could see what he was doing: *focussing* on a sense instead of thinking or noticing other senses—but I suggested that he should try to feel rather that he was *opening up* to a sense so that it becomes so overwhelming that nothing else interferes.

For example, at one point he heard a motorcycle and thought: "That sounds like a big bike."I suggested he should be more aware of all the sounds within that noise, as if he had never heard anything like that before, leaving less room for thought. His response was:

> I can now understand what you mean about that. Try to be open, experience, but not "put any labels" on anything I'm hearing. Just consider them as alien sounds. I repeated this part of the exercise yesterday. It's amazing what a difference this does make! Being as much unbiased and detached as I could, I could feel like "living the moment" better, so to speak. That was great! Later on, when the Dagger started its analysis, it was sort of too late, since the experience had been registered inside already. I'll definitely do this exercise again.

Another person apologised: "I did end up succumbing to my analytical mind at times." My reply was not to worry about that: the long-term objective is not to eliminate analysis but to get a good working relationship between analysis and receptivity—so that analysis can step back and allow receptivity to reap, then step in to sort the wheat from the chaff. Without some analysis there can be delusion, and the fear of delusion is one of the main factors that blocks psychic powers.

WHAT SHOULD I DO IF I NOTICE SOMETHING REALLY NASTY?

One person wrote:

> When I walked through one particular place I got an unusually strong kinaesthetic response, which seemed to be because it wasn't a very nice-looking bit of street. It didn't feel very nice, but the rest of the experience was very pleasurable.

Another put their negative experience more vividly:

> Smell is a problem for me. Since my pregnancy all my smell neurons got turned on. I would nearly faint from the smell of bleach and blood in the butchers section at the back of the supermarket. It's easier now, six years later... The Awareness walk, not good to do in the inner city, the tree-lined path behind the fairgrounds was littered with used condoms, a human turd and copious human and dog piss. Some small buds on the trees give off a faint green whiff, and the cars all give off different choking smells... It's impossible to keep it up. I retraced my steps a few times, but gave up and carried on. I came back slightly overwhelmed.

Of course, this was one reason why I suggested a walk in the country or in a park—not that nature cannot offer her own share of grisly experiences, but rather because for most people today the country holds fewer vivid associations. (On the other hand, a keen bird watcher might find the wildlife so dramatic that they would do better in a quiet street!)

What I suggested to this person was to work at the "not-naming" state. Again, a question of pure observing rather than thinking and labelling: so you do not see "a turd" (let alone a "human turd"), but simply a brown muddy pile glistening with moisture. No recognition, naming or judging occurs; merely sensory impressions with something like a Buddhist state of non-attachment.

I agree, however, that it is one thing to do this with visual impressions, but much harder when hit by a more visceral sense—such as smell! Dog shit is a pretty tough one, but other more removed "bad smells" lend themselves to a sort of re-framing.

Notice how differently some people react to common country smells such as horse manure—an unwelcome smell, but not as threatening as dog shit. Country people going into a stable are more likely to take a deep breath and say something like, "Aaah, that's good healthy horse-shit." Doing that, they are opening themselves fully to the experience by filling their lungs with it. The opposite reaction is to cringe away from the smell with hand over nose and say, "Uuugh". People who do that tend to remain disgusted for much longer. From the Dagger point of view, you could say that because horses only eat grass, horse shit is not so threatening to us humans, and so we do well to get used to it. But dogs and cats eat meat, and so their shit could more likely contain germs harmful to other animals, including humans—and that is why it is not so easy to adapt to that smell.

A similar principle applies with nasty noises. When a very loud and unpleasant sound like a noisy lorry or jet disturbs me, I have a tendency to shrink and cower as if trying to keep it out. But I was advised that it is better to imagine that one is completely transparent to the sound and let it wash right through me. I've tried this approach, and do find that a more open awareness leaves me feeling less hurt than when I allow my defensive "cutting off" reaction.

I Have Too Many Mundane Chores And Distracting Moods To Let Me Get On With These Exercises

Another writer said she was slow getting started on the exercises because of being swamped with mundane tasks like her "toilet training laundry nightmare currently overwhelming my thoughts (and mood)."

I suggested that heightened sensory awareness can be used to help us face up to unwelcome chores. You might think the secret would be to reduce sensory awareness, so that you were less aware of the nasty job, but an experiment I carried out as a schoolboy proved otherwise.

I described how I was appalled at the prospect of knowing I had promised to clean the car, but was feeling utterly disinclined to do it. I just wanted to stay inside in the warmth and not be messing with buckets of water. So, rather than setting out to clean the car, I set out to perform an experiment. The object of the experiment was to find out why I did not want to do the job—to discover what exactly it was that was so repellent about cleaning the car.

So I began by filling a bucket of soapy warm water, concentrating on the precise physical sensations and my reactions to them with the question: "is this act of finding and filling a bucket the thing I so dreaded?" No, it didn't feel that bad. Then I took a sponge in my hand and plunged it into the bucket asking, "is *this* the part I could not face?" No, it wasn't that bad... and so on. At each step I moved to the next stage of washing the car and concentrated on being aware of all the sensations and feelings to see what was so bad about them. Eventually the car was completely cleaned and I had to admit that there was not one single action that was so unpleasant as to justify the sense of dread I'd felt.

Rather like the approach to human turds, I was forgetting that I was "cleaning the car" and instead focused on physical sensations. Before I did this experiment, all the thoughts about not wanting to clean the car had built up, like a dark genie, into a mighty oppressive force of resistance.

But when I turned the activity into an experiment, the genie faded away and I was left with a clean car!

This same technique of focusing on the senses rather than labelling our experiences can be a very useful way to handle unpleasant moods or feelings. For example, you might one day be frightened of a coming exam, or feel sick with love or sorrow. The normal thing in those circumstances is to get locked into cycles of thought—"Oh, why did I do that? I feel such a fool, I feel sick with shame," or whatever. Each time you find yourself describing your inner state—e.g. "I feel sick with shame"—stop labelling it with words and instead ask yourself what are you actually feeling in your body? What is the actual sensation? Does it feel like a weight in your heart? Or a tightness in your throat? Or what?

This process can be the beginning of a healing of the condition. For the full story of how to do it, see my previous book *Uncle Ramsey's Little Book of Demons* (2005).

WHAT SORT OF RESULTS SHOULD I GET FROM THE MUSIC EXERCISE?

I was pleased how good the results of this exercise were. Everyone reported quite strong feelings as to which bits of music were best heard in which position—I thought some might still have thought it a silly question.

Looking back, I believe it was an excellent starting point because music plays so strongly on our senses, even though it is mostly heard and only slightly felt as vibration. People had quite vivid impressions of what the music was doing once they started listening in this wide open way. Here are some examples :

> After a couple of minutes I could start to feel the bass drum travelling from the speaker, in through my mouth, down into my legs, and then back out again. I tried to imagine the sound waves coming at me from the speaker like somebody breathing them out and blowing them over into my direction... Lying—I did this in the same location as I was sitting, moving the chair. Immediately, I was aware of the sound flying straight over my head onto the wall behind me and bouncing back. The sound felt somewhat distant, as if it was coming from a place much higher than the celling of the room. Standing—again I was very strongly trying not to hear individual sounds, but the whole piece. This time, the sound seemed to bounce off my midriff, refusing to enter my stomach. For me, the music seemed to sound best whilst standing; I felt I could hear the "whole" of the piece.

> When she hits the high notes I could really feel it within my cranium and through my shoulders. The bass line was less easy to detect, along with the drums, guitar and organ music. I listened to the song again

> standing up, and this time I could feel the bass line vibrate from the soles of my feet and upwards towards my pelvis. I could feel the sound of the drums and guitar in the solar plexus area. Duffy's high-pitched vocals still had the same effect from the shoulders upwards. It was as if standing up made my body more "open" to the music somehow, since I was still facing the stereo."

HOW DID PEOPLE GET ON WITH THE OTHER EXERCISES?

I received only one comment on the wine tasting exercise, but it was a joyful one:

> Then came the magic moment of wine tasting. I really enjoyed this part of the exercise. In fact, I was pondering how different things would have been if I'd had exercises like this at school. However, I reminded myself that I had to stop thinking and concentrate on tasting. So, I opened a bottle of Italian Valpolicella. A nice reddish, pinkish, not deep red colour. The smell was nice, typical of any red wine—I couldn't tell any difference. But the taste was quite another matter altogether. A lightly fruity and sweet taste with a bitter after-taste. It was giving me a pleasant, euphoric feeling. I was feeling some warmth in my heart. Then I was having something like a vision, inks of

> different colours falling, diluting and morphing into water. Every colour was a different "sub-taste", so to speak, and in the end they were all mixing up to the colour of the wine, contributing to the overall experience.

One participant got a non-sensory visual experience even in this first week—seeing things moving beyond the field of vision was the sort of experience I would only be looking for in the fifth lesson.

> Then, switching to vision, I focused on the ground in front of me and noticed a piece of paper blow in the wind and spiral across the ground and how people stepped to avoid it without thinking. I kept my head very still and it passed into the periphery of my vision, and I became aware that there were people moving around behind me. I couldn't actually see them, but I could "see" them as human-shaped blobs, somewhere in my head—like stars appearing and disappearing during a planetarium display. There was a moment of dizziness and I then felt the breeze on my skin as it gusted over me and blew through my hair, setting my scalp tingling as I abruptly became aware of my position and chair. It was as if (to use an analogy) somehow I had become aware of the "impression" I was making in the soft,

> almost doughy substance of the world, if that makes sense?

I mentioned above how one writer told me of a shamanic extension of the sensory awareness exercise—the senses as animals. Here is another very interesting variation that can be practised as part of the course:

> The Ambiance Exercise, to open your sense of ambiance. Basically you remember every time you walk through a portal of some sort to check the ambiance. Eventually you get so good that you can sense the ambiance change when someone else walks into the space you are in. Even if you can't see them you can sense what colour clothes they are wearing. It's good to do this exercise consciously, you pick up many things on what is happening around you—allowing any presages to flow in easier too.

One final comment, just to underline the sheer value of these exercises quite apart from their role in expanding awareness and developing clairvoyance. One participant apologised for being slow to get going on the exercises because of a busy schedule, then added:

> That said, even reading the exercises reminded me of the importance of beauty as the natural counterpoint to drudgery. And anything that enhances our sense of beauty

can only, in this age of plastic and general grimness, be a good thing.

A Sense Of Place

In the first lesson we began by exploring very subtle sensory data—sounds sights, tastes, smells and feelings that we know to exist but are usually too subtle to be noticed or acknowledged.

In that first lesson we deliberately didn't try to go for clairvoyant or psychic perception, because that might provoke resistance from the rational parts of our mind. The other reason was that, if we did get clairvoyant phenomena early on, they could excite our curiosity so much that we would be tempted to concentrate on those results rather than learn to open up to *all* impressions.

This week we go a little further, building on last week's last exercise to see how well we can read subtle bodily reactions.

You know how you can sometimes walk into a place or situation and think, "This feels bad (or good)"? If the bad atmosphere feeling is strong enough, it might put you on your guard, or even make you decide to get out. We now want to extend awareness and look a little deeper into those hunches and see if we can develop them further.

IS THIS REAL CLAIRVOYANCE WE ARE EXPLORING NOW?

Not really, though it is on the borderline of real psychism. In normal life, when we get these hunches we are too busy to do much about them, so we only tend to register the stronger messages—"I *love* this place!" or, "That bar gives me the creeps"—and when we look back the outward signs might have been pretty obvious, such as a beautiful location, lovely view, or on the other hand a dark and dingy atmosphere.

But if we explore further the signs are less obvious. Why does one bright and cheerful café excite me while another one does not? Look hard enough and you'll probably be able to pin down some significant difference—maybe it's the tree outside, or the waiter's friendly manner? But however much you try to eliminate all those obvious factors, often some elusive quality still remains. There is "something about the place" that attracts or repels you.

That's what we are looking for, that elusive quality that we sense about a place or situation, and first of all we are going to make an effort not to analyse it, but to perceive it. Not the Dagger, but the Cup.

EXERCISE 1: FINDING YOUR OWN PLACE

This exercise is very basic and quite adaptable. Go to a quiet space, preferably outdoors and not too familiar, and wander around in it, maybe practising heightened sensory awareness, looking inwardly at your feelings and bodily sensations, as described in Week 1, Exercise 5, until you find the spot where you are most comfortable. Do that several times in different places and then try doing the same exercise in an indoor space.

Why do I recommend you start in a place that is not too familiar? Because if it is a familiar place (such as your own garden), then the chances are that you will have already more or less consciously have found your own spot within it.

Why do I recommend that you start out of doors? Because that gives you more space to wander in, and there is likely to be more variety to explore.

Why do I suggest a quiet place? So that the choice of your own spot is not overridden by some obvious factor, such as trying to get as far as possible from some noisy machinery or children.

WHAT DO I MEAN BY "FINDING YOUR OWN SPOT"?

If you don't immediately grasp what I mean, think of it this way. Stand in the open space and imagine that you have arrived early at a garden party, where you know nobody. What is the natural thing that people do in those circumstances?

Imagine that you have just been handed a drink and so you wander into the area, feeling a bit shy and awkward. You don't want to stand right by the gate or door looking stupid, so you wander about, maybe pretending to look at the garden, etc., until you find a place where you feel at ease to wait for the party to warm up. Without being conscious of it, you have "found your spot".

With reference to last week's description of the Cup and the Dagger: the process of finding your spot is Cup-like. You do not analyse what you are doing mentally or lay down any criteria ("I must find somewhere quiet, with a good view, and some sun") but rather you tune into your body and your senses, as I described in the first lesson, and look inwards for a feeling that the place is comfortable and right for you.

It's more a process of moving through space and looking inwards at how you feel, than looking outwards at the place itself.

HOW DO I KNOW WHEN I'VE GOT IT RIGHT?

Repeat this exercise in a number of different places and situations until the sense of "finding your own place" becomes familiar and natural. You'll probably find you get quicker at recognising your spot.

Remember, in this exercise we are not doing anything very new. We are only doing something consciously that we normally do naturally without thinking about it. Notice how often in canteens and bars the regular customers will be found sitting in the same place each time. They could sit anywhere, but often they gravitate to their favourite spot, and can even feel irritated if someone is already in their place.

EXERCISE 2: EXPLORING FENG SHUI

When, and only when, you have become familiar with the idea of finding your spot, then it is interesting to turn to the Dagger way of thinking, and start analysing what are the factors that make this "yours".

The chances are that you have chosen a slightly raised place, or one giving a good view of the area, yet not too obviously on the highest point; it may be pleasantly in the sun, if the weather is cool, or shaded if the weather is hot, and so on.

At an indoor party the chances are that your spot will be away from the entrance, yet with a clear view of it, where you will not catch the eye of people entering, but be at a about a 30 degree angle to the door.

What you find, basically, is that you choose a place with good Feng Shui.

Feng Shui can seem such a bizarre art when you study all the traditional strictures as to what is a good or a bad place to build a house, or to site things in a room. But I was told that when wealthy European colonialists first started living in the Far East and having houses built for them, the native population could not believe that they did not know about Feng Shui. Why? Because they mostly built their houses in the best spots anyway, the ones with the finest Feng Shui. They were simply choosing places that they felt would be nice to live in.

The lesson is that, when you are rich enough to be able to build just where and how you want, the choice of what "feels right" tends to be pretty close to what the rules of Feng Shui would recommend.

This can be a useful tip for anyone learning about Feng Shui: don't just think about it as a set of elaborate rules, but feel the significance of those rules and how often they make sense. For example: it is bad Feng Shui to sit at an office desk with your back to the doorway; so imagine being at such a desk and how disturbing it can be when people enter the office behind you and you cannot see them without turning round. Place a mirror that gives you a rear view of the doorway, and you may feel more relaxed.

EXERCISE 3: BODY AWARENESS

For the next exercise we work a little more on inward awareness, starting a sort of dialogue with our own body in order to tap its wisdom. Again, this is close to clairvoyance, but can easily be seen as just being more sensitive to "real" bodily sensations in order to pick up what the body needs.

Begin by being aware of your own body and its subtle reactions, as described in Week 1, Exercise 5, and the "Finding Your Place" exercise. But this time we are not asking how we react to a place, as in Exercise 1, but how we react to food—or rather, the thought of particular foods.

Let us say you are in a restaurant looking at a menu that describes the dishes in reasonable detail. Something like: *Grilled sirloin steak with wild mushrooms and a green pepper sauce served with crushed potatoes and sprouting broccoli.*

Instead of simply reading the words, or looking at the price, to make your choice try to imagine actually eating it. First, imagine grilled sirloin in your mouth—that should not be difficult unless you are vegetarian. Then imagine wild mushrooms—you have probably had those at some time. Then imagine them together, with pepper sauce. This is more difficult, unless you've previously had this restaurant's pepper sauce and know what it tastes like. And so on, adding all the ingredients imagined as best you can.

Meanwhile you are listening for your body's reaction. Is there a slight hint of nausea? Or an eager watering of the mouth? Is there a feeling of "nice but not today, thanks." Or is there a feeling of acceptance without full satisfaction, as if something is missing? In that case ask yourself *what* might be missing and try to imagine the taste of that too—an accompanying glass of wine, or some bread maybe? See if they complete the picture.

This sounds like a slow process, and it may well be at first. In practice you needn't run through the whole menu as you can eliminate certain items immediately and narrow down your choices to one or two. With a little practice you can do this quickly, and it becomes an automatic habit. And so what if it is slow? Good eating deserves time and this way you get the pleasure of eating twice over!

Practising this has been very easy for me and it increases awareness of how the body responds. I find it hard to sympathise with those who say things like, "I know I shouldn't eat it but can't help myself" or, "I've ordered far more than I can manage", when the body usually expresses so clearly what it wants.

Nor is it just a matter of initial choices: the wine might be superb but, when the waiter comes to fill your glass again, just re-savour it in advance and see if the body really does want more. People who practise this are less likely to end up drunk, because the body simply reports what it needs, rather than what you think you should drink to be sociable, or to show off.

With practice, this exercise can become so natural that I wonder why everyone does not do it. My conclusion is not that other people's bodies are dumb, but their voice is drowned out by the clamour of other voices. People order a dish because it is trendy, or the most expensive or cheapest on the menu, or because their diet demands it, or because someone else has ordered it, or because it is visually interesting or quicker to prepare. People have second helpings out of habit, or politeness, or because they did not notice the glass being filled, and so on.

Moralists who rant against the body claim that carnal lust leads to excess, but I do not agree. If you really listen to the body it knows exactly what it needs and when best to stop. Excess has more to do with non-carnal abstractions such as status, pride or duty. Hunger certainly is carnal, whereas greed is a corruption of spirit.

The above exercise in eating food in advance is just the beginning of a new way of living. Practise it and you become aware that there is a principle within our bodies, reflecting millions of years of evolution, that not only knows what it wants, but also makes wise choices. Get to know this principle, and you can use it for self-healing.

For example: let us say you are feeling ill, maybe tired and nauseous. Instead of immediately reaching for a painkiller, look into and explore the physical sensations of the illness—don't label them, just feel them, where they are and what they feel like. Then, while you are doing this, think of possible remedies and imagine the feeling of those. How would I feel if I took a walk in fresh air? Or if I were to lie down? Or to drink a glass of water? Or take an aspirin?

Explore these possibilities and you may get a strong feeling that, yes, this is what I need. Act on that hunch, and it is very likely to be what you really do need—it just feels right and it works.

Remember that for millions of years our bodies have evolved without the help of pharmacies and doctors. You see, for example, how a cat with a stomach ache goes out and does something quite untypical, such as chewing grass. It is following an instinctual wisdom that we have forgotten to listen to, because we have so many alternatives now.

Your body may not have the up to date research skills of the pharmaceutical industry, but it knows itself better than any examining scientist. So begin by asking what it needs, listen to how that does or does not help the condition, and then at the very least you can go to your doctor or pharmacist with a clearer report on your condition and what you have already tried.

SUMMARY OF WEEK TWO

In Week One we began by exploring very subtle sensory data. In order not to provoke protest from our rational faculties (the Dagger) we did not aim for psychic data, only for stuff that we knew must exist, such as small acoustic differences or subtle tastes just outside normal perception.

This week we extend that exploration by going for something that sounds a bit fey and psychic—"finding one's true place"—and then we look back at what we find and maybe discover that the result is actually quite sensible. We explore using pure inner feeling or intuition (the Cup), then we examine the results and find that they are pretty good from the Dagger's point of view.

The object is to teach the Dagger to trust the Cup. In our culture we are often taught that only reason and analysis can be really trusted, and that we should never jump to conclusions or act on impulse without careful consideration. That is not bad advice, but it does limit experience, and restrict psychic powers.

If the Dagger learns not to be so suspicious of feeling and the Cup, it is less inclined to jump in and take over every experience. One of the big blocks to psychism is that inner voice saying, "I *should* be feeling this," or, "I can't possibly be feeling *that*".

Our object in this course is not to discard or demote the Dagger, but to make it wait until we get results. Once we have results, the Dagger can play a vital role, helping us to sort out which are useful and reduce the risk of delusion.

The confidence you will attain when the Cup and Dagger are working well together is a great help, because the fear of delusion is the second big block to psychism.

QUESTIONS AND COMMENTS

What sort of inner feelings should I be looking for when exploring to find my place?

That's what you might call "the wrong question", because you would do better to wander around and see what feelings arise in you, rather than setting out to look for a particular feeling. Everyone has their own response; for me it's often a sort of calm "centred" feeling in the belly. However, I will give some examples from people on the Arcanorium course.

Several of them had done a similar exercise in another context—finding one's "place of power" is a basic exercise you learn on shamanism courses. I avoided using the phrase "place of power" because I did not want readers to begin with any assumptions as to whether they should feel powerful in that place or not. Indeed, if you decide to go further with this sort of exploration, you might even decide that your "place of power" is not the same as "your spot", where you simply feel most comfortable. Take my example of the ideal party spot, where you can see who is coming in, but are angled so as to be not directly confronting the door: someone of a more dominant nature might find that for their place of power they chose to confront the entrance straight on.

One participant said that when they go looking for a power place, they work on a very visual level—if they have difficulty finding the place, they visualise ribbons of coloured light, and then those ribbons seem to converge on a spot that turns out to be right for them. Another said their physical sensation was of heat: as they approach the right spot, a heat builds in the stomach and then moves up. Once it reaches their head and their ears start tingling, they know they've arrived.

Another also felt heat. On arriving at a circle of concrete in front of a statue, the person noticed a feeling that the wind had dropped. Everything was dead quiet, and they suddenly felt a kind of warmth coming all the way up from the feet to the navel. It was such a blissful feeling, they closed their eyes and savoured the moment. It didn't last long, as they soon heard voices and people arrived, but they knew they'd found the right place.

One participant with shamanic experience noticed an unusual number of buzzard sightings on the way to their place, and saw that as a significant sign, as the buzzard was their shamanic "power animal".

Doing the exercise at home, one participant whose usual favourite spot was on the staircase, decided that this was partly a conscious choice and so began searching the house in the way I described. The discovery was a completely new spot under the stairs in the living room.

DON'T THE RULES OF FENG SHUI MEAN THAT EVERYONE SHOULD END UP CHOOSING THE SAME SPOT?

If you consult a Feng Shui practitioner with a very precise question such as, "Where is the best place for me to build a house on this plot?", then you might get a very specific answer identifying just one spot. But if you ask a vaguer question, such as "Where in this garden are places with good Feng Shui?" you will probably be shown a number of places. Although people looking for "their spot" will tend to gravitate to those places, there will still be plenty of individual variation.

These variations might reflect a more detailed study of Feng Shui. For example, instead of "Where is there good Feng Shui?" you could ask "Where is the Feng Shui best for me?" and get a narrower set of choices from the expert. He might even say, "Because you are a Metal Dragon person, you should choose this place..." I do not myself know enough about that subject to analyse any further.

Several participants noted what I had said about the angle of vision when you find your right place. One said that when they started analysing the place they'd chosen, "I had positioned myself in line with the main street in the town and also so that I could see when there were people approaching from all directions. In the canteen it was near the door, at an angle." If that angle is important in choosing a good place, there will be a whole line of spots which make the same angle to the entrance, and some people might still prefer to be close to the door, and others further away.

The one who found a favourite place at home under the stairs said that they could watch the garden from the window and the patio door, and experienced a mixed feeling of security and enjoyment of good views. They also made an interesting observation about the stairs being at a forty-five degree angle above their head: "I remembered an article somewhere that some people prefer standing near sharp wall angles and some near obtuse wall angles in their home. There were theories about house or wall configurations shaped in a pyramidal, trapezoidal form, etc., and the effect of these configurations on human psychology." This might also play an unconscious part in finding a place that feels right.

HOW CAN I EXPLORE THE MENU THE WAY YOU SUGGEST WHEN I'M WITH OTHER PEOPLE AT THE TABLE?

I did explain that this can at first be a slow process, but with time it becomes almost immediate and instinctive. One participant said they always had trouble making minor decisions, having Mercury in Libra, and sometimes took ages over a menu because, "What I do is exactly as you describe, experiencing each possible choice before deciding". But, as they pointed out, it does not have to be practised in a restaurant, you can always just look in your fridge and use the techniques to decide what to cook—or you could use it while browsing the grocery shelves.

But there was at least one who found it difficult in a restaurant. They reported this was partly due to concentrating on the conversation, "Trying to get the jokes in my non-native language," but also because, being something of a gourmet, he always wanted to try everything.

In his case their was a further problem I had not thought of. He was a Greek, and the custom in Greece is not so much to make individual choices from a menu, as I suggested, but rather to start with a big shared plate of everything—multiple dishes of meat, fish, salads, dips etc., and each person takes their plate and fills it with bits and pieces from the different dishes.

The answer is that the same basic technique could still apply when simply choosing from a shared spread: look at each item and mentally taste it before piling it into your own plate. It's a very simple basic idea, and you can adapt it to most circumstances.

WHAT IF YOU ARE ON A DIET? MIGHT THE TASTING EXERCISE TELL YOU TO EAT THINGS NOT RECOMMENDED?

Going back to the last participant, from Greece, he described how, even in other countries, he tended to get his partner to order a different dish so they could taste each other's choice. But, as he concluded, "I end up having most of mine and a significant portion of my partner's meal. Then the euphoria stops and the bloated feeling begins".

That bloated feeling is the sort of effect that the exercise can help to overcome. As one participant said: "I found that the body awareness exercises kept me from eating when I'm not really hungry. I realized that a lot of the time, I just snack out of boredom, or because I really like the taste of something, and not because I'm that hungry. I always suspected this, but this exercise kind of confirmed it."

More specifically, another said: "I broke my recent chocolate habit when I did the exercise and realised, with a watering mouth, that it was actually an orange I wanted. I'll definitely work more on this one."

So the exercise can become a sort of diet in itself—one that asks the body what it really needs rather than laying down arbitrary rules according to some general theory of what is good for people.

However, if you are on a diet that you really trust, then the question is this: how rigid is the diet? If it leaves you no choice, and you are committed to that diet, then the exercise becomes irrelevant. But if there is some choice—one lettuce leaf or two—then you could still make the decision in the way I suggest.

MIGHT THE TASTING EXERCISE ALSO BE USEFUL WHEN SHOPPING FOR FOOD?

Food marketing companies and supermarkets send out a lot of strong marketing messages designed to overrule our natural appetites and lead to bad habits. A survey by Visa suggested that the British spend on impulse £83 billion in cash every year—some £33 per adult, per week—and that this mostly happens when shopping for food.

One result is that £8 billion's worth of food is thrown away in Britain every year—amounting to one third of the total we buy, according to the Government-funded Waste and Resources Action Programme. In 2009, over Christmas alone, 230,000 tons of food worth around £275 million was just thrown away! This is not simply food that has gone mouldy or has passed its eating date: most of the 6.7 million tons of food we jettison each year is still perfectly edible.

If more people practised the tasting exercise as they walked the supermarket aisles, and asked if they really wanted to eat the stuff, it could significantly reduce that wastage.

But Can We Always Trust Our Bodies To Make Those Right Choices?

When I originally described this exercise in *Uncle Ramsey's Little Book of Demons* (2005), I made it clear that, when we consult our bodies, we are consulting an expert. Expert opinion should always be listened to, but it is up to us whether we act on it.

If you felt depressed and your doctor told you to go and eat rat poison, would you do it? No. If a doctor's advice seems very wrong, the normal thing is to get a second opinion. As I pointed out in that book, it is ironical, but slavishly following an expert's advice is not a sign of respect, it can even betray passive aggression—you ask a policeman to help you cross the road and he tells you to go hang yourself, and then he finds your body hanging from a nearby lamppost. Big deal!

So when your body says it wants to eat this, or not eat that, you can be sure it has some good reasons, but that does not mean they are always right. I myself know that my appetite can be skewed when I am sick, but I still mostly trust my body when it says it does not want food, rather than obey well-meaning people who want to see me eat. But I realise that some illnesses could seriously mess up the choice.

As one participant explained: "I found I had to be careful sorting what my body wants from other interferences. The hormone imbalance craves sugar and comfort-foods, and then occasional candida takes over my brain and wants sugar, so it takes a while to sort out what is coming from where. But that kind of listening is important work to do for health."

She added another interesting point: "As a mother of a young child, I think you mostly have your senses open a lot of the time. It's a mother's protective sense." She went on to say that, as her child was getting older, this awareness was fading a bit. So she decided to test her instinctive awareness by deciding what toy to take before taking her son to a friend's house. She instinctively picked up his wooden sword, but then reason cut in: "I cant arrive at someone else's house with a wooden sword!" However, it turned out that the child they were visiting was passionate about knights and had swords, helmets and shields galore!

CAN THESE SORT OF EXERCISES MAKE A MUNDANE PLACE OR EXPERIENCE SEEM MAGICAL?

Yes, indeed!

As one participant put it: "Tomorrow, I will go around the grounds and sense my spot. One might not think of the grounds of a council flat as being loaded with magical potential, but there was something about the place when I first saw it, before I was even able to get inside the flat itself, that felt good. So, among tomorrow's plans is that overdue exploration."

Go for it!

Dowsing And Divining

In Weeks 1 and 2 we explored the direct perception of sensory stimuli at the edge of normal conscious awareness, pushing the boundaries by looking for subtle information (such as slight acoustic changes or a feeling of place) that would normally be screened out by reason and convention. After all, who would want the embarrassment of being the only person standing up in a formal concert? Or who would go hungry rather than be seated in "someone else's place" in a restaurant? Rather than acting on such subtle preferences, we go along with the crowd and prefer to act normally.

The result is that we do not ask these questions, such as "Where do I really want to sit?" because the answer might be inconvenient or embarrassing. Have you noticed how awkward it can be sometimes when one person is over-helpful and, rather than simply letting everyone sit down as they arrive, they make a big fuss about,

"Wouldn't you rather sit here with the nice view?" Mostly, we'd rather just move with the crowd than make a big thing about small preferences.

Having pushed at those boundaries, this week we explore them from another angle, using a pendulum as an instrument. This could achieve several things: firstly it might provide information too subtle for even the extended senses we practised last week; secondly it might for some of us provide clearer or quicker answers than trying to feel directly.

Don't Dowsers And Diviners Use A Forked Twig, Or Bent Coat Hangers?

Yes, they use all sorts of things, from bare hands to elaborate spring-loaded devices such as the Cameron Aurameter. Basically, they are all just ways of amplifying the tiny unconscious movements of the hands so as to be easier to read their signals.

For simplicity, however, I'll only be describing the use of the pendulum, because it is easy to make and understand. The same basic exercises can also be done with forked twigs, horizontal pendulums, bent coat-hangers, etc., so by all means use those instead if you are happier with them. The best reason to choose a particular divining tool is because it feels right and works best for you. That is why, in the second exercise, I suggest some personal choices regarding the pendulum.

SO, WHAT IS A DOWSING PENDULUM?

The pendulum is a small weight at the end of a short string, chain or thread. It could be a purpose-made pendulum, or something like a blob of blue-tack or putty at the end of a piece of thin string, or a key on its chain, or whatever.

The length of the string I suggest should be somewhere between a finger or hand's length—the longer it is, the slower it ticks. String or thread may be better than a chain, which prefers to swing in a single direction because of the way the links are formed. The weight at the end can be any shape, but it helps if it is pretty symmetrical. A more pointed tip (like an inverted tear-drop) can be helpful when dowsing over a map, diagram or list of words, because the point makes for more accurate indication.

The picture shows how to hold a pendulum. Hold the string as shown and let the pendulum hang down from your hand so it can swing freely.

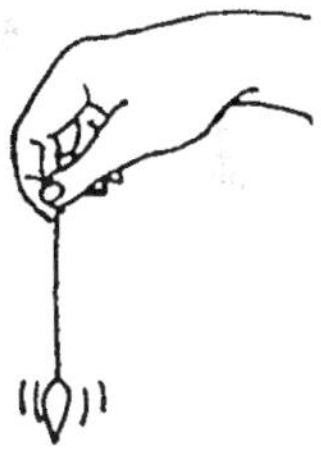

The first step is to establish a language for communication. I suggest three basic types of communication—answering yes / no questions, indicating direction and finding a place. Some people try to insist that there is one correct way the pendulum communicates, but in most people's experience it is a matter of seeing what works best for yourself.

How Do I Ask Yes/No Questions?

The usual convention is: rotate clockwise for YES, anticlockwise for NO, and to-and-fro for DON'T KNOW.

So, set it swinging to and fro and ask a question with a definite YES answer—such as, "Is my name [your name]?" or, "Is today Monday?" on a Monday.

The pendulum should begin to change from a to-and-fro to a circular clockwise movement, indicating that the answer is YES. Repeat the experiment a few times using other questions with obvious YES answers to make sure it always works, then choose a deliberate NO question, such as "Am I ten feet tall?" to check that it rotates the other way. Then mix YES and NO questions to make sure it always swings the right way, i.e. that the language is consistent.

If you find that the response is consistently wrong—such as anticlockwise for YES—then you need to experiment with anticlockwise for YES and clockwise for NO to see if that is consistent.

How Do I Get The Pendulum To Show Me A Direction?

There are two common approaches. The first is to set the pendulum rotating in a circle and ask, "Where is [known object]?" and watch it begin to take up a to-and-fro movement along a particular line. So, you might stand in sight of your house and say, "Where is my house?" and the pendulum will begin to oscillate along a line pointing at the house. Note that the to-and-fro motion gives a straight line, but does not tell you whether the direction is forwards or back along that line. So what you then do is move to another place and ask the same question to get a second line. The answer will be where the two lines cross.

This method—finding two lines and seeing where they cross—works quite well for finding a place on the map. For example, you lay out your map on a table and begin with the pendulum at the edge of the map, and ask something like "Where is my house?" to get one line. Then you take the pendulum to another edge and ask the same question and get another line. Where the two lines meet is your answer on the map.

The second method is to ask the question with the pendulum swinging to and fro, then slowly turn around pointing the other hand in front of you. When the pendulum starts rotating in the YES direction, you take it that your hand is now pointing in the right direction.

HOW DO I GET THE PENDULUM TO FIND A PLACE?

One method has already been described, finding a place on a map. Let's say we had asked, "Where is my place of power on this map?" and the pendulum has lead us to a particular place—how accurate is that answer? It depends on the scale of the map. Next, we go to the actual place and ask the same question, so we can narrow down the search to a particular spot.

One approach is to do the same as we did on the map: ask the question in two different places, get two lines and see where they meet. The other is to use the other technique, pointing your finger and finding what direction you need to walk in. Having obtained the right direction, you then let the pendulum swing to and fro along that line and walk slowly in the direction indicated. When you reach the right spot, the to-and-fro swinging changes to a YES rotation.

If I Need More Instruction, Where Can I Find It?

It is very easy to use a pendulum, much easier than it is to explain in words. But if you want more instruction a Google search will produce plenty of results.[1]

Some websites do get a bit complicated, or are trying to promote and sell a particular type of pendulum, so don't be put off.

I've Heard The Pendulum Can Be Used To Find Lost Objects—Will We Learn That?

One of the biggest problems with using the pendulum is that it is so easy for conscious thoughts to influence the pendulum's motion. It can become simply an indicator of what we already know or expect, rather than providing any new information.

Although one of the most useful things you could do with a pendulum is to dowse for a lost object, I do not recommend that you begin along those lines. Nor do I recommend starting with tests like getting a friend to hide something under one of several cups and dowsing to discover which one. In all such cases the "lust for result" is too strong, especially with an onlooker to impress, and you may find your mind rushing ahead with, "I bet he hid it under the sofa cushion, that's where I'd put it, and that cushion on the right looks a bit rumpled..." and so on. Once you start expecting a particular answer, sure enough the pendulum starts swinging towards that cushion.

So, in the first exercise, I suggest you experiment with deliberate cheating, to get the feel of what cheating feels like and how it works.

EXERCISE 1—USING AND ABUSING THE PENDULUM

The only thing we really need for this week is to be able to locate a place or answer a yes/no question. So, using the techniques I've already explained, take a pendulum and establish a language for yes/no, for leading you in a certain direction, and for telling you when you have found the right place.

I suggest that, having got the basic language sorted out, you explore the relationship between thinking and the pendulum's movement. Ask the pendulum where something is when you can already see it—and note that it points that way. Ask a question where you *want* a YES answer, and see it give that answer when you mentally say YES. And so on.

The idea is to become familiar with the way the mind interferes, so you will become better at allowing it *not* to interfere.

When you get used to using the pendulum, it really does seem to act independently of our will and produce surprising answers. Sometimes people using a forked twig are convinced that the twig has a will of its own—it really feels that way—yet reason says it must all originate from tiny movements of the hand.

So give reason its due, explore the boundaries of reason, then work with the story that it is actually the pendulum teaching you.

EXERCISE 2—ADDING RITUAL

The following exercise can be bypassed if you think it is not needed.

It's just that, with some people and some forms of divination, a level of formality or ritual gets better results. So—although any old pendulum should work—you may feel better getting or making a very special one and maybe charging it in a ritual manner.

Myself, before I ask a question about, say, my health, I begin by holding the pendulum on a short string then gradually let the string slip through my fingers so it effectively gets longer, and I note when the pendulum's swinging is most vigorous, and use the string at that length.

By doing this, I am effectively "tuning" the length of the pendulum to suit me each time. A New Ager might describe this as "adjusting the pendulum to my energy level", or "tuning it to my personal vibration". If that sort of language suits you, it can help a lot. But if it makes you puke, avoid it!

Then I will ask, "May I ask questions about my health?" as a sort of formal politeness. Doing this little ritual prepares my mind and focuses it for the questions to come.

If you like the idea of using a little ritual like that, it will help you to get into the mood for dowsing

EXERCISE 3—THIS IS THE REAL THING FOR THIS WEEK

Okay, we've got the preliminaries sorted out. Now for action.

What we are going to do is reduce interference from the rational conscious mind, *by asking questions that are meaningless in its terms.*

Instead of taking the map of your local area or town and asking "Where is the train station?" (which is like looking for a lost object when you have a pretty good notion of where it might be), instead you ask the pendulum, "Where is this region's heart chakra?" or "Where is the spiritual centre?" or some such question—just as long as you have not already decided where the region's heart chakra is!

In a small area like a garden you can do it direct on the ground, but in a bigger area like a town it is good to start with a map spread on a table and use the pendulum to locate a rough area on the map, then go to that area and use direction to locate the actual place on the ground.

This is a lovely exercise! It leads you to some odd discoveries, and is a great way to get a new perspective on the place where you live.

What I find is that, even though a question such as "Where does the main line of spiritual energy run in my town?" sounds meaningless in hard rational terms, the pendulum always leads me to something that is in some way interesting, thought-provoking or illuminating.

When a group of us in an ancient town in England asked "Where is the town's creative centre?" we were lead to not one but two places, and both turned out to be nature reserves. When I asked (using more direct clairvoyance than the pendulum) why we'd been led to two places, I received the answer: "A man has only one creative centre, and that is his head; but a woman has two: the head and the womb." A curious, but quite an evocative response.

WHAT SORT OF QUESTIONS MIGHT I USE FOR THIS?

Example questions that allow the pendulum to lead you to something interesting without a lot of rational intervention can be along the following lines.

"Lead me to the:

1. nature centre
2. light centre
3. dark centre
4. fountainhead
5. the [whichever] chakra, or
6. the place of power."

Or, "Find me:

1. a ley line,
2. a line of energy
3. a line of light
4. an etheric vibration, or
5. whatever."

You can also extend Exercise 1 of the previous week by asking something along the lines of, "Lead me to my true place of power in this town". Or simply use the pendulum instead of direct intuition (as described last week) to find "your place".

The key thing is to choose something that:

1. you do not already know;
2. does not have an obvious material or rational correlate;
3. or one that is meaningless in rational terms.

When you find it using the openness of the Cup, then I invite you to inspect the results using a little of the Dagger (as in last week's Exercise 2), and you may well find that you have been lead to something quite interesting.

Exercise 4—Dowsing For Diet And Health

Another useful practice, following on from the Week 1 exploration of body-sense, is to use the pendulum for advice on health and diet.

As we are still exploring the boundary between reason and intuition, let me again suggest a rational justification.

In the second exercise this week, we found how easily the pendulum is directed by the mind. Even when we try to hold our hand still, the yearning for a certain answer tends to move the pendulum that way. Even an unconscious desire will effect the result.

Now, the body has evolved over millions of years to cope with extreme dangers and changes, and diseases and different diets. So it must have gathered immense wisdom. If we hold the pendulum over some food that is likely to harm us and ask, "Is this good for me?" the body probably knows the answer better than our conscious mind.

It is also likely that the body knows the answer better even than a trained nutritionist, who knows a lot about the general rules of nutrition, but not so much about what is actually going on inside your own body at that moment. So allow the body to manipulate the pendulum and give an answer.

You can use the pendulum in this way to advise you on diet, or on cures, or to help you make decisions when you go shopping.

WHAT IF THE PENDULUM RECOMMENDS SOMETHING VERY WRONG?

Some people might ask: "But what if the pendulum tells me to swallow arsenic?" Then simply do the same as you would if your doctor told you to swallow arsenic—get a second opinion!

In the comments on the last lesson I addressed the question: "Can we always trust our bodies to make those right choices?" Look back at what I said there.

SUMMARY OF WEEK 3

I began by describing the use of the pendulum, then I drew attention to the problem of conscious interference with the results.

Next, we set out to bypass this interference by asking questions that were meaningless in everyday terms, using the pendulum to lead us to something unexpected, and then looking at the results.

Expect to find something interesting about the place you live in. I'll be surprised if anyone gets absolutely nothing from doing this. What I hope you will be left with, is a great way to explore a familiar place and form a fresh new relationship with it.

For the first time in these lessons we are truly exploring phenomena that lie outside the realms of reason. This is where real clairvoyance begins!

QUESTIONS AND COMMENTS

There were not many participants who had the time in one week to get out and explore their district , but we did obtain some interesting and enjoyable results. The idea of bypassing the rational mind by focusing on a question that was meaningless created a lot of discussion, and threw up some interesting ideas for practical magic.

DO YOU HAVE ANY OTHER SUGGESTIONS WHERE I COULD FIND OUT MORE ABOUT DOWSING TECHNIQUES?

As I suggested, this is not so much a course in dowsing as a lesson on using very simple dowsing techniques to encourage more general psychic powers to develop.

If you Google for dowsing instruction you'll find a mass of websites and books, many of them excellent. But some books and websites are advocating a particular dowsing technique, laying down the law—"This is how to do it properly"—as if there were only one right way, or only one proper tool to employ. What we need is an experimental approach—"Let's see what works best for you"—so that we can explore and discover psychic powers we never knew we possessed.

So, for this course, I recommend only those sources that take a similar experimental approach. For a really good, undogmatic but sound introduction to dowsing, I'm a great fan of Tom Graves and his original book *The Diviner's Handbook* (1986).

A simpler text, especially suitable for this course as it focuses on the pendulum, is *Elements of Pendulum Dowsing* (2008), also by Tom Graves.[2] Another simple course by Walt Woods, called *A Letter to Robin* (2001) was found and recommended by one of the participants.[3]

WHAT SORT OF PENDULUMS DID THE PARTICIPANTS USE?

They mostly did not say. One had a couple of nice crystal pendulums from a New Age shop, another tied a piece of string to a keyring tag with a nail sellotaped onto it pointing downward to make a more precise pointer. That person found that the shape made a difference:

> I tried the calibration procedure by swinging it to and fro, and then clockwise for YES, and

> I've had no problems at all. However, on the anticlockwise NO movement I've had some difficulty. The circular movement was somehow "stuttering". On better inspection I saw where the fault lay: the ring that connected the keyring tag with the string was triangular. After replacing it with a circular ring, there were no more problems.

Another experimented with the length of the string:

> I found the optimum length was about ten inches. While I was gradually lengthening it, I was asking the question "May I ask about a location?", getting prepared for Exercise 3. It was at ten inches that the pendulum started swinging clockwise, answering YES.

HOW CAN I EXTEND THE IDEA OF "MEANINGLESS QUESTIONS"?

My intention, when I suggested beginning with questions that had no meaning to the rational mind, and so would avoid rational interference, was simply to help the beginner obtain some results without conscious interference. Once you start to get results, it increases confidence, and then you can move on to more testing questions and other types of psychic power.

But several of my participants—and remember that Arcanorium College has many practising magicians attending its courses—saw this as an interesting technique to help with general divination.

One of the issues that arises when practising any form of divination based on random input—tarot, teacup fortune telling, I Ching, for example—is whether you should concentrate hard on the question as you shuffle the material, or whether you should make your mind blank. What many say is that it is better to make the mind as blank as possible during the actual selection, because too much "lust for result" can bias your choice. Even though the shuffling should result in a random choice, if you are too intensely involved in the question it might somehow bias the resulting spread.

As one participant put it:

> I've never felt that I had much of an ability to do deliberate divination, maybe because I always tried to rely on merely keeping the question sort of "in the back of my mind" whilst divining, but of course it always seems to intrude to varying degrees.

So, what this person suggested is that you could get the best of both worlds by putting the question in the form of a *sigil*—that is, a symbol made up from the question but that from its appearance has no obvious meaning. You then keep your conscious mind busy, but distracted, by concentrating on the sigil while you shuffle.

As an example, you could use the sigilisation technique used by the English magician Austin

Spare: write down the question in capitals, then cross out all repeated letters:

> What ~~a~~c~~t~~ion sh~~o~~uld ~~I ta~~ke~~ in order to~~ g~~et the~~ j~~o~~b?

That leaves the letters:

> whatconshuldkergjb

You can arrange those letters into a pretty pattern on a piece of paper. That pattern will be meaningless and yet, because of your concentration in creating it, encapsulates the entire question in hidden form.

So, while you shuffle the tarot pack, swirl the tea leaves or count the I Ching yarrow stalks, what you can then do is focus intensely on the shape of your pattern. The question will not be on your mind, and yet it will be lying just beneath the surface of your consciousness.

HOW FAR CAN I TRUST THE "TESTING FOR HEALTH" ANSWERS FROM THE PENDULUM?

We had some interesting responses when people tried using the pendulum to test food. This first one carries a useful message about making sure you are precise in the question you ask, and do not let wishful thinking cloud the answer.

> I took one of the delicious but deadly little biscuit pastries that a friend (despite my

> pleas not to leave them) had brought for tea. Having already scoffed a couple of these melting little petits fours, I waved my pendulum vaguely over the last one: "Yes" my pendulum said, "Go on". But it can't be, these really can't be healthy at all, are you sure? "Yes yes yes!" it said, without hesitating. Then I realized the question I had actually been posing was, "Will this harm me?" Of course it will!

Another person noticed a difference when he used the pendulum over food in or out of its wrapper:

> I experimented on a cereal bar. I used the pendulum while the foil wrapper was still on, and the pendulum seemed a bit ambivalent—it just wasn't moving. I removed it from the wrapper, and the pendulum started swinging in the YES response.

This a good example of how one might be tempted to be dogmatic and lay down a rule: "When testing food, make sure it is not in its packaging!" But our minds are smarter than that, they can distinguish food from the box it comes in. In this case, the mind might have wondered if he was asking if the whole thing, food plus wrapper, was to be eaten. But it could equally have simply wanted to see the bar before deciding Have you ever had the experience of buying some prepackaged food that looked good on the label, but when you opened it your stomach sank in dismay?

So the lesson here is not cut and dried. Just experiment and see what works best for you.

Another participant used this technique to choose remedies, such as the Bach Flower remedies. It helped fine-tune the recommended quantities, because—after all—when the bottle says "Take one tablet three times a day" the manufacturers do not know how much your body actually weighs—are you a two hundred pound rugby player, or a one hundred pound marathon runner?—and how sensitive are you to medicines? Your body might prefer just two, or even one a day.

I myself have used the pendulum when choosing Bach Flower remedies, and I've noted how the answers were a combination of two things: sometimes exactly the remedy I would have chosen by consciously matching the remedy to the condition, but also remedies that it would not have occurred to me to choose. What was interesting was that, if I found that something unexpected had been suggested, when I looked it up and really thought about the diagnosis, it invariably proved relevant. It was not what I had expected but, when I looked back at the textbook, I found myself saying "Of course! Why did I not think of that remedy!"

Just as a warning, in case you think this is all too easy, I'll quote another participant who had perverse, yet quite consistent answers:

> I performed this exercise with mixed results. By swinging the pendulum on different foods and asking the question, "Is this good for my health?" I got positive answers for foods like coffee and croissants, and negative for foods like fruit and yoghurt. Yes, I am aware that there is something wrong here. I don't think it has to do with the pendulum's calibration. I must admit that I didn't allocate enough time on this exercise. I have to repeat it properly, constructing a list of all the different foodstuff in my kitchen, and dowse them multiple times, marking the overall percentage result.

Yes, more work was needed on that one!

WHAT SORT OF PLACES DID THE PARTICIPANTS FIND THEY HAD BEEN LED TO?

One participant began with an Ordnance Survey Explorer map—a good choice as Britain, more than any other country I know, is blessed with very good maps with superb definition and features that are really good for dowsing. This person had previous experience with dowsing, so chose to begin with dowsing rods, then use the pendulum to narrow down the spot. He found two spots when he asked for the "Heart Centre", and drove to visit them.

At one spot there was private woodland on each side of an old track way that wound through fields and woods. He kept checking that he was on the right track and for a while thought that maybe his question was not specific enough: "Maybe that *whole area* was the heart centre rather than a specific spot?"

From my experience, that is quite a common issue. The map, especially if the scale is not large, may take you to quite a nice area, and you arrive wondering if this was your whole answer, or if you are supposed to find some unique spot within it. I would suggest it is always worth continuing by dowsing on-site and to locate one specific spot that is—in this case—the "heart" of the Heart Centre.

Sure enough, he finally came to a spot that felt right, even though it was a totally nondescript place of scraggy hedgerows where the footpath branched on the brow of a hill. He then used his rods to check out the spot and decided it marked an area about ten paces across. As an experienced magician, he then performed a small ritual to honour the spot.

That is a lovely thing to do, if you know an appropriate ritual. Otherwise I would suggest just sitting or standing in the place you have found and experiencing it with the sort of "opening the senses" meditation described in the earlier lessons. Think of the phrase that you used to find the place—in this case "the heart centre" and just sit and feel or "listen to" the place.

He also noted that there was a farm near the spot called "Summer Hill". What was interesting was that was also the name of the other place he had found on the map. He commented, "As I approached both sites in the car my awareness became sensitised. Dowsing raises consciousness, for me, far quicker than meditation—it's virtually instantaneous."

Another person tried two different pendulums and also found two different places—in a town, on this occasion. She asked for "places of power", expecting to receive sites of ancient archaeology in her historic city, but this turned up, to her surprise, a couple of spots both of which had connections to recent occult or alternative groups—one a converted church where rituals had been held; the other a pub where a group met regularly. She wondered if her conscious mind were bringing about these results, especially in the case of the pub—but it is worth noting that consciously she was expecting an ancient site of archaeological significance, and the pendulum had insisted on something different and yet thought-provoking.

As a further example of the odd results you can get from this exercise, another person asked for the spiritual centre of Milan in Italy. She got three results on the map, and took the bus to visit them. Getting off at the first spot she was face-to-face with a place called "Buddha Bar". Sounds a bit spiritual doesn't it? Well, in her own words it was: "A monument of crass superficiality and a typical haunt of the Milanese. Maybe it was not so far off then, because money is definitely the main object of worship in this city."

Note the teasing ambiguity here: you ask for the spiritual centre of a place that is highly materialistic, and you are lead to a place that encapsulates the spirit of materialism. I did say that the pendulum will take you to somewhere that is thought-provoking!

On the one hand you could say that this was an example of the pendulum's wisdom, revealing the true spirit of the place. On the other hand you could take it as a lesson that, if you want tangible results, you need to ask better-defined questions. In that case, do not forget the whole object of this exercise was not the finding so much as the searching—I was deliberately asking for vague questions, so that the emphasis was on exploring your abilities, not doing a test to see if the pendulum "works" according to some test criterion.

On the third hand—if you have third hand—you could say this result was a lovely example of how the Trickster can tease one with intriguing but off-key results when you start experimenting with psychic powers. Have fun, but keep your hand on your mental wallet, as it were!

So, what were the other two places she found? The second was a tall chimney at the Military hospital crematorium, replete with crows: "I had to laugh; a direct line to heaven!"

The third took her to the other side of the city, right onto the outskirts in an industrial area. She found a doorway with people walking in and out:

> Wow—I thought here it is! I followed them through the small green door and found myself in Chocolate Heaven! It was the Tre

Marie factory shop. Tre Marie make very high quality chocolate and pastries, what luck! The first thing I laid my eyes on was the strangest thing, a packet of off-cuts from Catholic hosts, basically thick rice paper. How useful! Still, I think my pendulum has a fine sense of humour. I didn't know I had it in me! But it was great fun and I think next time I will try for more useful things, like a spiritual centre which is relevant to me.

It is indeed a great way to get to know your area from a new angle.

Playing With Tarot

When I named the original Arcanorium course "Clairvoyance For The Non-Psychic", it was not so much that I believed some people to be psychic and some not, but rather that some are less sensitive to intuition or "psychic" information than others.

From my experience, the reason for being less sensitive seems to be that other faculties drown out or overwhelm the psychic data, rather than there being no psychic data to work on. For some people it might be strong feelings that overwhelm the psychic messages: for example, there are religious people who feel that anything psychic is diabolic, and this feeling is so strong that it blocks psychic impressions. I did not expect that reaction from anyone who chose to study an Arcanorium course, but I did expect some of them to have interference from the rational mind. People attracted to chaos or "post modern" magick often approach from a rational standpoint, and that was why I put so much emphasis in the first three weeks on building a more co-operative relationship between the busy mind and intuitive impressions.

The rational mind can interfere in several ways, firstly as the purely negative equivalent of the religious protest against psychism: instead of the belief that "this is evil" there is the equivalent belief that "all this is unscientific nonsense!" Another form of interference, less negative but just as blocking, is sheer curiosity. Here the mind becomes so involved that it drowns out any results: "Gosh! the pendulum really is moving! I wonder how it does that? Is it my hand moving?" Then there can be a fully co-operative mind trying too hard to be helpful and interfering by helping intuition along—such as when trying to find your place of power and you find yourself thinking, "Look at that lovely sunny mound over there, that would be a really good location to find my place of power..."

But the biggest block of all is when the rational mind and the feelings combine to take everything very seriously: "I know there are a lot of bogus fortune-tellers out there so, if I am to become a tarot reader, I must make sure I become a *proper* one and not a charlatan or self-deluder". The very desire to do our clairvoyance properly, to not be a fraud or charlatan, becomes a block against getting any results.

In my early years I bought several tarot packs, hoping to suddenly discover one that would leap to life in my hands and seem to speak to me, but I struggled because the symbols of the twenty-two trumps in particular are so complex and rich in associations that it was hard to see how to combine them into a meaningful reading. I did much better with astrology where relatively (I repeat, *relatively*) simple symbols, encapsulated in keywords like "energy" for Mars, are combined into complex structures. The structure of a tarot spread is much simpler than a horoscope, but the symbols themselves are so complex.

So, this week we will tackle that sense of over-seriousness head-on by exploring two very playful approaches to the tarot, ones that could help anyone who so far has "tried too hard" to break through into a more relaxed and intuitive relationship with the cards.

EXERCISE 1—STORYTELLING WITH A TAROT PACK

Materials needed:

1. A fully pictorial tarot deck, like the Rider/Waite drawn by Pamela Coleman Smith, where every card has a picture rather than an abstract diagram. In many packs only the trump and court cards show people; pip cards such as The 4 of Swords just show a pattern of swords. But here we need all the cards to show a scene.

2. You also need a three year-old child. Sorry, I didn't warn you about this in my

> introduction, because I know it takes some 3.75 years to make one of these items. But you can do the exercise with your own three year-old Inner Child instead.

This is what you do: when the child asks for a bedtime story, you take the tarot pack and solemnly shuffle it—"This is the maturity of man, when he regains the solemnity of a child at play" (F. Nietzsche)—then lay out four cards face-down from left to right. (If you do not have a child to hand, then get yourself into the mood of a three year-old refusing to go to sleep until you've been told a story.)

Then you intone the magical invocation. "Once upon a time...", turn over the left-most card and simply describe what you see. Example (2 of Discs): "Once upon a time... blah blah... there was a funny man with a red hat who danced and practised juggling with two golden plates... blah blah... he had come a long way from those far distant mountains, dancing and juggling all the way..." Note how the imagination begins to embroider into the narrative—the "blah blah" bits are as much description as you wish.

Then, as you run out of ideas, turn over the next card, which might become an explanation of the first, or the next development. Example (Queen of Wands): "Why was he travelling and juggling? Because he had fallen madly in love with a beautiful queen sitting on a throne and he wanted to travel to her court and impress her with his juggling skills..."

That is all there is to it: instead of using the tarot to "do a reading"—with all the seriousness and significance that might entail—you simply use it to make up a bedtime story for a little child.

I suggest a three year-old—actually it would work for any age, but a three year-old is content with very simple stories and does not demand anything clever. As a child gets older we might again begin to become too serious, thinking "I'd better come up with a really good story, or they'll complain that I didn't read them *Harry Potter*." The whole point is to remove the sense of seriousness and be solemnly playful.

I suggest four cards as that worked well for me: it allows an initial scene-setting, then a development or bit of background, then a decision or course of action, and a final outcome—all that you need for a simple child's story.

I discovered this idea when I had my own toddler who wanted bedtime stories. I found it very easy to do, and began to realise that I was no longer struggling to invent a story, as they soon started jumping out from the pictures. I had at last begun to do readings without really trying.

Also, as you practise this simple story-telling exercise, you will find the stories flowing more and more easily, and becoming increasingly intuitive. You are on your way to becoming a tarot reader, without trying too hard.

Thanks to this exercise, I got over my early resistance to reading tarot and have since moved onto the Crowley/Harris tarot. It is more abstract and so less suitable for children's stories, but is a beautiful and inspiring set of images.

EXERCISE 2—YOUR OWN "TAROT" DECK

Even those who are already skilled with tarot readings might find this a refreshing exercise.

I suggested to the Arcanorium students that they collect a variety of postcards in the few weeks leading up to this lesson. I suggested aiming for twenty to thirty cards at a minimum, and choosing a pretty diverse set of images with distinct, strong themes.

By this I mean not twenty long-shot landscapes, or twenty pictures of crowds but a mixture—say, a postcard of a cathedral, of a hill-fort, of a pretty flower, of a car, of a train, a ship, a mountain, an office block, a busy street, a beach, a humorous card, and so on. By all means include several in the same category, as long as they are distinctive—e.g. a sports car, a family saloon, a hearse.

In this exercise we will use that set of postcards as a tarot deck and will do readings with it. Because the images are unconventional, and because you may only have twenty to thirty cards to chose from, I suggested a pretty basic tarot spread using just five cards placed in a cross with the meanings shown opposite.

So, think of your question, shuffle the cards in whatever fashion you are used to, then deal out five cards face-down in the order shown, starting

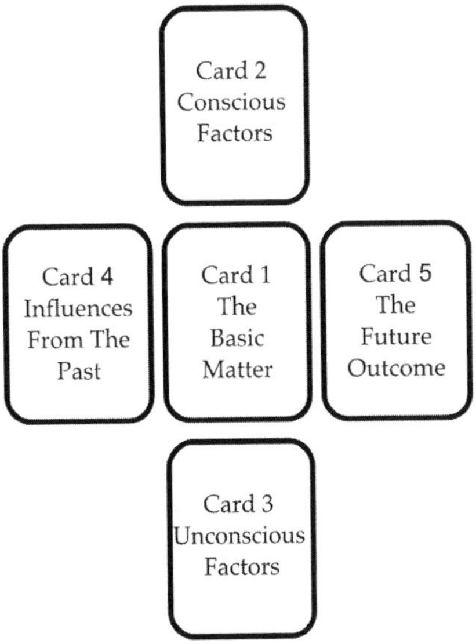

with Card 1 in the middle, then the second card above it, and so on. Turn them over one by one and interpret accordingly.

Let's imagine you asked: "Will I find the job I really want this year?" The first card you turn over, "the basic matter", shows a picture of a motorbike on an open road. What does that picture mean to you? You know it means (let's say) "freedom". This suggests that the question about finding a good job is really about an anxiety that getting a job might restrict your freedom.

Card 2, "conscious factors", is turned over and shows a Picasso print and the word "creativity" jumps into your mind. Yes, consciously you want a job that offers an outlet for your creativity.

Card 3, "unconscious factors", shows a picture of St Paul's cathedral. To one person that might say "City of London" and suggest that, deep down, you actually are more concerned about your financial situation; or to another person it might say "religion" and suggest that, although wanting to be creative, you have an inner need to know your work is ethical or godly. And so on.

Of course, they don't have to be postcards if you have old photographs that are suitable. You could cut them out of magazines—but it is easier to shuffle and deal something like a postcard.

What is nice about this postcard tarot game is that:

1. It is a very personal tarot, because you yourself have collected the cards. It is generally considered that the very best tarot is one you have created yourself—postcards just make it a lot easier!

2. You are also inventing your own interpretations—for example, an office block might symbolise "work" or "success" or "slavery" or whatever, on different occasions, just as the motorbike might mean "travel" or "haste" or "danger" as well as "freedom".

3. This tarot pack can be quite up-to-date, and feel relevant to modern life, because the images will often be contemporary.

4. Above all, this tarot reading is playful, because it is a collection of stuff you found rather than anything that belongs to any serious occult tradition. It is your choice, your responsibility, and there is no-one to say you are reading it "wrongly".

EXERCISE 3—BEYOND GAMING

A few weeks before the start of the Arcanorium course I received an e-mail from a reader of my books who wanted to ask some questions and in return sent me a link to a paper he had written. I was delighted, because what he wrote tied in rather neatly with the content of the course, and he said he'd be quite happy if I drew my students' attention to it.

The title of the paper (The JuanKurse, 2007) was: *Practical Proto-Topology of the Divinatory Mind or, An Occult Examination of the Use of a Board Game to Enhance or Develop Mental Divination which is Without Tools or Equipment.*[4]

Its relevance to this lesson is that the practice described uses a board game for a number of reasons, including the emphasis that this puts on "play". Indeed, the author says we should choose a game that we enjoy playing. He also suggests it must be one that is not so simple that you can easily work out winning tactics with your conscious mind (such as noughts and crosses, or tic tac toe), nor must it be so complex that you cannot yourself get a grasp on strategy (such as chess or go, to the non-expert). So, draughts or chequers might be a good compromise, but it should be a game of strategy, not chance.

In essence, the technique is to play the game against a human opponent and choose your moves "intuitively" rather than by thinking out a strategy. Here are some further suggestions the author gives:

1. Formulate an initial wish, for example "I will win this game."

2. Don't focus on parts of the board, but rather gaze at the whole board with a bird's eye view.

3. When choosing a move, look at a piece and picture the move, but focus on your inner feeling in the way described in earlier exercises—does this move feel right? Actually, the author suggests that we refine the search by seeing what sort of inner feeling goes with best results in the long term.

4. Keep playing, and see how your clairvoyance develops.

5. When you have developed a reasonable level of skill, start applying the same technique in the more complex game of life itself.

SUMMARY OF WEEK 4

In exploring the interplay between intuition or psychic sensitivity, and a busy mind that can drown out the former, we examined the tarot pack.

Here we found a set of symbols in relationship, and we expected our intuition to weave them into a relevant and useful narrative that cast light on the original question. That was asking quite a lot, and it is hardly surprising that our minds were likely to step in and try to take control.

I addressed the difficulty by suggesting a more playful approach. Firstly by simple "storytelling"; and secondly by using informal personal symbols rather than calling on some Great Tradition or a recognised set of cards. These are two ways to practise and gain familiarity with tarot-reading without being too serious.

As a third exercise I drew attention to some work on using a board game to develop clairvoyance in a similarly playful spirit.

QUESTIONS AND COMMENTS

THE CUP AND THE DAGGER REVISITED—A SHORT INTERLUDE

How well are you progressing so far with developing your psychic powers?

In Week 4, did you slip fairly easily into the playful spirit that allowed you to make up stories with the tarot cards and then read interesting and useful meanings into your collection of pictures?

Or are you still slipping back into mental busyness, questioning whether this is "real", getting over-excited by "results", or simply trying too hard?

Early on I introduced the metaphor of the Cup and the Dagger—a magical metaphor used to describe two mental states. With the Cup our minds are open, to receive impressions and simply hold them as a cup would, in their wholeness without division or analysis. Whether these impressions arrive from without—via our five senses—or from within as hunches, feelings or imaginings makes no difference to the Cup because its job is to receive and hold, not to classify or analyse.

With the Dagger, however, we are mentally sharp, looking intently at an impression and giving it a name, analysing it, classifying it. So, to the Dagger, it makes a big difference whether something comes via the senses, or whether it comes from within as a hunch or imagination.

For the Cup, when we tell a children's story using tarot cards, it is meaningless to ask whether the cards gave us the story, or whether it was made up by our imagination, all that matters is how well the Cup's contents taste—whether it is a good story or not. But for the Dagger, the distinction is all important: "That wasn't a real tarot reading because I just made it up!" Even if it was a good story the Dagger could say: "Okay, it was a clever bit of imagination, but it was still just imagination".

Remember that by advocating a Cup state of mind, I was not claiming that the Cup is in any way "better" than the Dagger. These two states of mind are equally valuable, but they each have their place and time. If there is an unbalance between the two, it lies partly in our education and society, where the analytical Dagger is seen as being somehow more "grown up", and so superior to the Cup. "Imagination is for children", whereas Dagger skills need to be taught at school and university, because they are what is needed for "real life". An artist or poet uses the Cup to earn a living, but unless they or their agent has plenty of Dagger-like business acumen, they will end up merely as dreamy drifters.

No, I am not saying "get rid of the Dagger" to become clairvoyant, but rather that we must learn to lay the Dagger carefully aside until we start getting results. Then keep it in hand while the results accumulate within that receptive Cup. Once we are confident that our psychic powers are working, that is when we should bring back the Dagger to separate the wheat from the chaff.

To give an extreme example, consider automatic or "channelled" writing (which I'll touch on in Week 6). Once you open the gates for channelling you often receive a huge amount of material, and usually there is an awful lot of drivel and flowery nonsense padding it out. For someone in the Dagger state of mind, that is reason enough to reject the whole lot as a load of humbug. However, you can also find among all the drivel some real gems—of wisdom or poetic beauty, or of both—that deserve to be treasured.

I have already explained this, so you may just think I'm repeating myself, but if you needed this repetition then it could mean that you are still having trouble keeping the Dagger under control. In that case, I will offer an alternative metaphor for you to work with. I will re-label the Dagger as "Left Brain" and the Cup I will call "Right Brain".

Right Brain, Left Brain—So That's What It's All About!

If you are now thinking, "So that's what it's all about", then beware! The reason I did not mention right/left brain earlier was because we are stepping into risky territory.

A metaphor works not because it *has* meaning but because it *conveys* meaning, as the word metaphor suggests. It is therefore a magical use of language. Cup/Dagger is a magical concept and so using them as metaphor is a magical use of magical language. But Right Brain/Left Brain is a scientific concept, so using it as a metaphor becomes a magical use of scientific language.

The problem with scientific language is that it belongs to the left brain, and so the process begins to be taken over by the left brain. This course then ceases to be a magical experiment in developing psychic powers and turns into a scientific experiment to develop right-brain thinking.

WHAT'S WRONG WITH THAT?

The problem is that a semi-scientific left-brain approach to psychic exploration leads to superstition in a way that magic does not. The reason that magic saves us from superstition is because it does not exist.

That statement, of course, is rubbish. Magic clearly does exist because we have just spent the last four weeks developing our own magical powers. But the point is this, although magic clearly exists, we all know that it does not *really* exist. That means there is always a spirit of play when we are doing magic, and the spirit of play is the best ever defence against superstition.

Science, on the other hand, is about things that *really* exist. So, if you start getting real results from developing the right-brain experience, it appears to prove that the Right/Left Brain metaphor must be *true*. Once you believe that, you are on your way to believing anything.

However—as the popularity of New Age pseudo-scientific books attests—there are many people who cannot get into magic without the crutches of scientific language, so let's totter forth in their honour.

WHY TWO BRAINS?

Sensory input from an animal's five senses is hugely complex. If the brain were to analyse all of that data thoroughly it would need to stop every few seconds and spend hours thinking through every moment of new experience. To get around this problem the brain has evolved two divergent functions. The right brain hemisphere is designed to accept the entire sensory and inner experience holistically, and we are aware only of a sort of overall feeling about that wholeness, like an animal on a prairie just standing there, feeling safe. But if something new happens—maybe some grass has moved slightly—this right brain becomes alert and makes a decision to ask the left hemisphere to investigate analytically.

For example: grass moving = wind? No, because nearby grass is not moving. Grass moving = hidden animal? Maybe, so let's focus around that spot to look for further movement and listen carefully too. (In Cup and Dagger terms, the Cup just contains the flow of experience and when something new drops into it, then it calls on the Dagger to fish it out and examine.)

The left brain feeds back its conclusions to the right brain and they merge to become part of the new wholeness experienced by the right brain.

So let's say we are in the prairie, we've seen grass moving and left brain has said, "Looks like snake movement," then the whole experience now contains an element of danger that will be felt as fear or anxiety by the right brain and probably result in further instructions being given to the left brain. When there is good co-operation between the two, the whole experience is held and then acted on as needed. Because the right brain has a better sense of three-dimensional space and movement it is able to take control and give the order to take action, unless (as often happens in our culture) the left brain has become dominant and tries to repress the natural reaction, leaving us dithering and confused.

It is often said, when humans first meet, that "first impressions are the strongest". People going for job interviews are advised that the impression they make as they first walk into the room will set the tone for the whole interview. That "first impression" is the right brain experience: a new person enters the room and something about them either attracts or repels us. After that we tend to analyse the person's appearance to justify our immediate judgement: "He knocked, but didn't wait for us to say 'come in'; arrogant manner; scruffy shoes, not making any effort."

In human society things can get out of balance, because language arises mostly in the left brain. Without direct access to language, the right brain experience is less often put into words, and when it tries to be expressed in words we struggle a bit and the best that language can do is use poetic or mystical metaphors. Sometimes, in the hands of an artist, this works well, but more generally the only experience that can be properly communicated and handed down in our culture is mostly left-brain experience. In the example of the job interview it will be the critical details that are noted in the interview report, rather than the feelings of the interviewer. When words are preserved in writing and lose the emotional undertones of spoken speech, left-brain thinking becomes even more dominant.

So, if you found my original Cup and Dagger metaphor a bit wishy-washy, and then your attention lit up when I mentioned the Left/Right Brain metaphor, then it is probably because the latter feels comfortingly familiar: "Ah, now at last he's talking sense!"

If that is so, you might get better results from the walking exercise in Week 1 if you reinterpret it using the brain metaphor.

The Total Awareness state I described—all senses alert and receptive, taking in the experience as a whole but not analysing it into parts, or naming what you see, or thinking about it—is a predominantly right-brain state. So the exercise can be seen as a way of reconnecting to the more primal right-brain world experience and developing it, without allowing the left brain to take over in its habitual fashion. If you are still finding it difficult to let your psychic powers flow easily, you should keep practicing the walking exercise and see it as a way to develop your right brain function.

COMMENTS ON WEEK 4

The story-telling exercise was especially popular, and it became a regular bedtime story routine for one participant's family, with the children also using the pack to make up their own stories.

The importance of starting with images of people became evident, because one person in particular got on fine with the story until the Major Arcana, or "Trump" cards appeared, and they proved too abstract to be easily interpreted.

This is a question of degree. Most of the Rider/Waite cards I used lent themselves immediately to story-telling, but I would find it much harder to do this with the Crowley/Harris tarot. This is the pack I use for tarot reading, but I tend to use it as many people use the I Ching, by looking up the interpretations in a book and then using the written word as the springboard for my imagination.

If I was not so busy writing this book, I would spend time practising direct story-telling from that pack, because it should be possible ultimately to tell stories (and so do readings) from *any* deck. The American mentalist Kenton Knepper has learnt to do a cold reading from a single ordinary playing card, a reading that might run along these lines: "You chose the four of diamonds—that's very interesting because diamonds are an investment asset and I sense a strong financial concern, reflected in the rather defensive square shape made by these four pips on the card. Of course, diamonds also signify beauty, and a commitment to marriage..." This shows just how much the imagination can pull from the simplest clues.

WHAT TAROT PACK DID YOU USE?

I was pleased by the number of different tarot packs that emerged, having only ever used the Rider/Waite pack myself for this exercise.

The first story posted on the forum was a wonderfully gothick tale of a mad scientist, wicked witch and black cat inspired by "The

Halloween Tarot", apparently based on the Rider/Waite pack but done in the style of a cartoon children's book. Another well-known pack was the Morgan/Greer, but among those that were new to me were the "Victorian Romantic" and the "Vampire Tarot".

Another participant introduced a tarot pack designed by William Gray, which they described as, "Very liberating in a serious, fun sense"—although I found the images too simple to fire my imagination.[5]

And yet another person had commissioned their own special deck, hand-painted in watercolours by an art student, using different ethnic styles for each element.[6]

DO WE PREFER POSTCARDS OR PERSONAL PHOTOS?

One participant had trouble with the story-telling and could not get the imagination flowing even in that playful context. But when it came to doing a reading using their personal collection of photos—they chose a selection of about twenty or thirty pictures—the personal meanings jumped out immediately: "It took a lot less thinking and meditating to come up with an answer to my question".

I could see how effective that sort of reading might be, personal questions being answered by old family group photos bringing up memories from the past. Whether those memories have a direct significance to the question—e.g. a photo of a domineering older brother in answer to a question about personal inadequacy—or whether it is symbolic would depend on the reading.

One participant commented:

> Some of the photos I dug out I had not seen for years, and I was surprised at the emotional reaction I had on my first glance at them. It is amazing how the sight of a knackered old TV set and paisley carpet from my parent's house ten years ago could elicit the kind of reaction that it did. I saw old friends, dead pets, and cringe-inducing past incarnations of myself. So I can relate to what you say about how old photos can almost be like parts of ourselves.

Several participants, however, had rather too specialised collections of photos. One said that a tarot made from her photos would be a new Cat Tarot, or a Goth Tarot if it included the pictures of her daughter!

As in the case of a too-abstract tarot deck, however, there is no real limit to what the imagination might still manage to create. Even thirty photos of the same cat might have sufficient differences in posture and activity to provide a reading—but if you are that good, why would you need to read this book!

At first glance, a collection of postcards might seem much less personal than your own photographs, but it depends how much choice went into collecting and keeping those cards. The chances are that each one would hold some special personal significance, and would have something to say in a reading.

One participant found their old photos just too emotionally-charged to be used for readings, but on the other hand commented:

> I really enjoyed doing a reading with postcards. I have been collecting postcards for years and have a lovely collection. I found the images to be immediately revealing, and it took the pressure off having to know the significance of the tarot cards.

How About Making A Game Of Everything?

There was an interesting correspondence concerning the final exercise in Week 4, using a board game to develop psychic powers. One participant wrote about his previous experience playing *Trivial Pursuit*:

> So when these questions came up I just kept my mind blank until the questioner, having read the question from a card, turned it over to read the answer and awaited a reply. In the split second that they read the answer I often seemed to get it too. This eventually became so apparent that they started making a point of not turning the card over to read the answer until I had made a guess.

"Psychic bidding", as a technique used when playing bridge, also came up. I understood psychic bidding to mean bidding on a hunch, but, on looking it up, the term seems to apply to a deliberately misleading bid rather than one based on intuition.

Someone had done a similar trick when playing *Cluedo.* Another game that came up was *Atomic Bomberman 4,* described as:

> A fairly old-fashioned puzzler where you move a "bomberman" through a grid-like playing field, depositing bombs in an attempt to take out the other players. If you win the game, a picture appears on screen of your bomberman (each individually coloured) holding a cup and celebrating.

What the participant did was to visualise a winning outcome, then use intuition to make it happen:

> In the seconds before the game started, I would go quiet, close my eyes and strongly visualise my selected bomberman in that "winner" image. When the game started I would mentally hold onto this image, and then play on impulse, without putting too much thought into my actions. I would be very relaxed about it, not holding onto the desire to win—simply maintaining a "zen-like" composure. And quite often I would win after doing this, despite my friends

being far more skilled and experienced at playing *Atomic Bomberman* than I was.

This raised the old but intriguing question about divination and enchantment: the sceptics say that when a witchdoctor predicts someone's death, it is the fear that it generates that makes the person die—so what seems to be prediction of death is really an enchantment to death. The extension of this argument is that, if you go to a fortune teller or do a tarot divination and what is predicted comes to pass, then how do you know it was a genuine prediction, rather than you creating the result because you believe that it will happen? The same participant went on to say:

> When I read the tarot to foretell events in the future, I often mentally focus on the day in question while shuffling and holding the deck. Usually I focus on its position on my time-line (NLP term) and picture myself looking through my eyes on that day, at the time and place. When I get it right, I assume that I made an accurate prediction. However, could it also be the case that on drawing the card, I had given my subconscious an alternate future to manifest? Or am I just making things more complicated than they need to be?
>
> I've heard of tarot readers using their cards in hoodoo-style magic candle-burning rituals as an enchantment. One magician I

heard of would draw cards for three alternate futures, pick the one they liked the best, and attempt to manifest that future in the ritual using the cards.

SO, WHAT WAS YOUR STORY?

Some of the participants posted their tarot stories on-line, and there was plenty of variety and imagination among them. Unless one had a copy of the same tarot pack they used, it was not easy to say how much was straight description and how much came from their own story telling.

So I'll leave you with just one example, chosen because it is a very simple one that shows how much the story can be based on a straight description of the cards rather than any great feats of creative imagination. Notice how the writer seems to be just describing each scene as seen on the card, and yet begins to read-in extra elements as the story progresses. Towards the end he speaks of the three travellers "seeking the remedy" and the lady and the old man "having confidence" that they will find it—in other words, the imagination is already beginning to fill in feelings and thoughts that are not directly written on the cards.

> Once upon a time, in the shade of a large tree, three beings meet. They have a mission; they are determined and resolved to fulfil

their task. One of them is young, and could be male or female, wearing a red cloak. The next is a large white horse who has an intricate gold and green harness. The third is a powerful bearded man, who is looking quizzically and serenely out of the scene. The horse is looking intently into the eyes of the person in red. We are at the start of something.

We now find ourselves in a mountainous scene with spindly trees. There is a glowing green orb hovering over a distant peak; in fact, the orb could be nearer and we are following it. The bearded man is riding on the horse. They have started on the journey and are walking into the landscape. The figure in red is waving a farewell, before following the other two, to a woman who is looking at him serenely while nursing a very pale man. They are in a place of holy sadness, beneath a soft green hill. They are at the foot of a simple wooden cross, which has a spear propped against it.

We now meet an elderly bearded man in grey-black. He has a red cross on the front of his tunic and red boots. Perhaps he is related to the earlier figure in red—he could be that younger person's father. He is holding a rolled-up scroll and a spear that is dripping blood. Is he responsible for the dead figure? He is standing within an ornate marble arch, where there are distant cloisters and a black and white chequered floor. The three travellers are seeking for the remedy to right the wrong that has been committed. The lady and the elderly man have confidence that the seekers will find what they are looking for—in fact it has already shown itself: the green glowing orb. So the chance of all living happily ever after is very possible, if nothing goes wrong on the journey.

Devas, Auras – The Great Arcanum

This is what the whole course has been building up to—the GREAT SECRET that will enable ANYONE to see fairies, devas, auras and a host of other clairvoyant wonders. SECRET KNOWLEDGE that has been jealously guarded by an exclusive cabal of priests and shamans since BEFORE THE DAYS OF THE PYRAMIDS. A totally new SCIENCE OF KNOWING that is, according to privileged sources, only just being developed in TOP SECRET CIA and RUSSIAN INTELLIGENCE laboratories and NEVER BEFORE REVEALED to the human race (except of course to all the above-mentioned priests, shamans, etc.).

Oh help... I hope this won't be one enormous anti-climax...

It is indeed a very simple trick and yet it made a great impression on me when I first stumbled across it after many years of unsuccessful attempts to develop direct clairvoyant perception. So I will make some effort firstly to re-create in your imagination the circumstances of my discovery.

After giving up on ever being able to see those Geoffrey Hodson devas when I was at school, I came across his book again many years later when I was regularly walking my partner's dog in a park. So I took to looking at trees and trying once more to tune into their auras.

Again I failed. Then one evening, as I stood gazing at an old hawthorn tree that had become a particular favourite of mine, I tried once more to see its aura in the dusk.

Before you read any further, please do the same.

From where you are sitting, is there any tree or plant, or a flower in a vase within sight? One that you can stare at right now? Or a mountain or river? Failing that, maybe a pebble or crystal or even a pet that you can look at to see if you can detect its aura?

For inspiration on what you might look for, here is Hodson's description, from a book about fairies, of his clairvoyant vision of bulbs in a bowl:

> In the examination of bulbs growing in bowls, it is observed that large numbers of small sub-microscopic etheric creatures are moving about in and around the growing plants. They are visible etherically as points of light, playing around the stems and passing in and out of the growing plant.
>
> They have the power to rise into the air to

a height equal to that of the plant, but I have not seen any rise further than that. They absorb something from the atmosphere, re-enter the tissue of the plant and discharge it. This process is going on continually, the creatures are entirely self-absorbed, sufficiently self conscious to experience a dim sense of well-being and to feel affection for the plant which they regard as their body. They have no consciousness apart from this.

When the process of absorbing is taking place they become enlarged and appear like pale violet or lilac-coloured spheres, some two inches in diameter, with radii of force flowing from a central point within the sphere. The ends of these lines extend slightly beyond the circumference. Having expanded to the largest size which they are able to reach, they return close to the plant, enter it, and begin to discharge the material, or vital force, which they have absorbed. The natural etheric vital flow from the half-grown plants reaches quite two feet above them, and in it other tiny creatures play and dance, tossed up and down by the flowing force in which they rejoice. To etheric sight they are less than a quarter of an inch in size, though both varieties must be sub-microscopic from the point of view of solid measurement.

In addition to this a process of absorption by the plants themselves is plainly visible, etheric matter flowing towards them from all sides. In some cases feebly waving tentacles are extended from the etheric double of the plant, and through them etheric matter is being absorbed. These tentacles are hollow etheric tubes, slightly curved and slightly wider at the mouth, and are pale grey in colour.

The longest I can see extends four to six inches from the plant and is from a quarter to half an inch in diameter.

And here are two of his pictures:

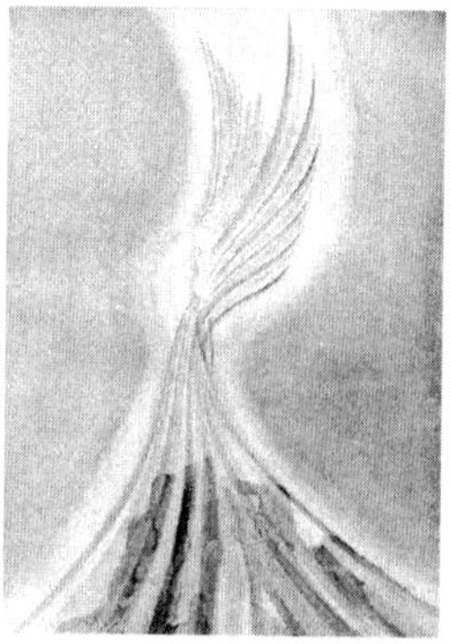

So: gaze for a while at the flower, or tree, or other natural object and try to see its aura or attendant spirit.

Some of you may immediately see it—if so, congratulations.

But this course is primarily written for those who cannot see it, and are waiting for THE GREAT ARCANUM.

EXERCISE—THE GREAT ARCANUM

When you failed to see the nature spirit or aura, ask yourself this question instead:

What am I truly trying to see?

In other words: "If I *could* see the spirit, what *ought* it to look like?"

When I gazed at my favourite hawthorn tree that night, and I asked myself that question, it came to me immediately that it really ought to have a deep crimson cloud-like aura with needles of golden light flashing through it. Then I turned to a nearby pine tree and knew that would have to be different—more like descending wisps of olive green and yellow. Then I looked at another tree and had a different, yet equally strong idea of what the aura ought to look like—if only I could see it.

Then I asked myself, "What am I doing?" Every tree I looked at, I could imagine what a suitable aura would be, even though I could see nothing directly with my eyes.

All the years I'd been trying so hard to *really* see a real aura, and failed. But when I asked myself what it *ought* to look like, the answer came quite readily in my imagination. Once I started to allow that to happen, it came easier and easier, and in a surprisingly visual imaginative form.

A voice in my rational brain said this was all nonsense—I wasn't really seeing anything, just fantasy. And yet it also struck me that this visualisation is in its own way very real—an interior designer, for example, looks at a scruffy room and can "see" what it would be like when re-decorated. They are not really "seeing" that, but the imaginative vision is clear enough for their client to pay them good money for that vision.

So what I suggest is that you go out into nature, look at favourite trees and plants and ask yourself what their auras "ought" to look like and see just how clearly you can imagine them. As you practise this, you will find the impressions begin to develop quite clearly, certainly enough to be able to describe and get an illustrator to paint them, as Hodson did.

If that still does not work for you, include some of the other game-playing techniques we have been exploring, such as:

VARIATION A—STORYTELLING

Imagine that you have decided to write an illustrated children's story about a little girl or boy who goes into a garden and meets the fairies. You want to make it nice and vivid, with good descriptions to fire the illustrator's imagination. So you go into a garden and stand before a plant—say a daffodil—and begin the story:

> One day little Louise was in the garden, gazing at a beautiful golden daffodil, when suddenly she began to see...

What do you think she might see? Picture what ought to be happening for little Louise's daffodil, with lots of detail to make it interesting for the story's readers.

VARIATION B—THE TRICKSTER

Imagine that you are on holiday, and have been latched onto by a dreadful pompous occult bore. He has overheard you mentioning that you are developing clairvoyant skills and he is frightfully intrigued. The more you try to shake him off, the more convinced he is that he has found a genuine member of the Inner Illuminati that he has read so much about.

He starts offering you money for clairvoyant revelations, and you are horrified. But someone has stolen your credit cards and you are indeed short of cash...

Go into a garden and imagine that he has again tracked you down, begging you to reveal what a Great Clairvoyant Master sees when gazing at this daffodil, and so you gaze knowingly at it with half-closed eyes and start to intone, "I see before me a humble daffodil, yet around it glows a..." Give him what he wants, in Spades. Then turn to another plant and pretend to see another aura. Then describe the Devic Lord of the Garden in glowing detail and so on.

Really pile it on until you almost begin to believe your own visions because they are just *so* good...

SUMMARY FOR WEEK 5

Sometimes we want something so much that we simply cannot let it happen. Like wanting to rebel against the limitations of material reality and reason, and to be able to do and experience "the impossible".

Relax, be playful, don't be afraid to cheat a little.

SOMETHING HAPPENS!

Don't jump on it and analyse straight away! Wait until you have gathered enough enjoyment to justify your little bit of cheating.

Then, and only then, analyse if you must—especially if you can thereby learn to analyse in a similarly playful spirit. Let the "left brain" have some fun too.

For a while I enjoyed this clairvoyant arcanum so much that I later wrote an article inspired by similar adventures, "The Charlatan and The Magus", which was republished in my collection of essays *Blast Your Way to Megabuck$ with my SECRET Sex-Power Formula* (Dukes, 2003).

I don't practise this much now, but every now and again when I'm in nature and want to tune in and be really nourished, then I look at auras, fairies and devas in this way and begin a conversation with the elementals.

So you can now return to the walking exercise in Week 1 and go for a walk in nature, getting into a state of total awareness, and then invite yourself to see the fairies and nature spirits all around.

It will feel good.

QUESTIONS AND COMMENTS

This is the shortest section, for the most important chapter in our course.

It is such a simple trick but, because it requires giving oneself permission to cheat, it could be difficult to get past the hurdle of thinking, "This is just fantasy. It's made up, not real clairvoyance". And yet, once you cross that barrier, it really starts to work.

I was quite apprehensive at the start of Week Five to see whether anyone would take the plunge and come up with results. So I was mighty relieved when the first post appeared:

> Okay, I've tried this one out, and obtained a few interesting results.
>
> The Small "root-stock" fig tree in my back yard—a small, Victorian style faerie, complete with butterfly wings, but blue, sleeping in the roots.
>
> The bamboo plant also in my yard—a Panda (obviously) with human eyes and a Chinese-style rice-picker's hat.
>
> The Nasturtium plants ready to go into hanging baskets—little green and gold children, dancing round the seed tray.

Terrific! Then there was a description of plants seen in a gated community near a busy road:

> All the plants devas had different "Urban" looks—the sharp-leaved giant grasses had

> various pierced punk-type looks. The Japanese Holly was an old beggar woman, wrapped in a tattered shawl and, over it all, a black pine tree was a regal looking woman, wrapped in a shawl, watching down on her "children", looking very sad.
>
> I then decided to branch out, and use this to see other spirits—in particular the gnomes living in the rocks scattered by the road. Very sad they looked, unhappy at being blasted out of a cliff, and straining to get back into the earth, where they belong.

Not everyone found it so easy, however.

> Not sure if I'm doing this right. While walking around and looking at trees in my locality, I found myself envisioning them in human terms—as in, seeing them as humans of various ages, genders, body types, etc.

In other words they were seeing human types as the previous person had done, but were judging that this was not correct, because they should be seeing colours and auras rather than people. They went on to say:

> Sometimes I would get a vague impression of a colour or quality, but other than that, I didn't see any auras. I think I may have lapsed into doing an exercise that I did ages ago from Jan Fries' book *Visual Magick*, which involved communicating with nature spirits

by using my imagination to personalize each natural object I came into contact with. I'm not sure if you are aware of the exercises in this book, but is that similar to seeing auras?

WELL, WHAT DO YOU EXPECT TO SEE?

This is the key point: do you have expectations of what clairvoyance should be?

The answer is mostly yes, because people take a course like this six-week course in developing clairvoyance with some idea of what clairvoyance means and some idea that they need to develop that ability and this course should help.

I played on that expectation in this lesson because I said that if you cannot see the deva or aura of the tree, then ask yourself what you are expecting to see. In other words: how will you know when you achieve clairvoyant vision, if you do not have any idea what clairvoyant vision looks like?

I then asked you to describe as clearly as you could what you *ought* to be seeing—I invited you to *imagine* what clairvoyance would look like if you were clairvoyant. Then, instead of throwing away that imagination, treat it as something of value and practise it several times until it comes easily. At this point you find you can look at any plant, tree, stone, mountain or piece of scenery and have a strong impression of what the aura or deva of that object looks like.

It might not be clairvoyance as you hoped or expected it to be, but what is that if not clairvoyance?

And What If It Was Not What You Expected?

But what if you get results, as the last person quoted, that do not fit your expectations?

This is interesting, because it suggests you are seeing something that you had not imagined you would see. Instead of seeing waves of colour, as in the Hodson examples, the writer was seeing people. But they felt that meant they were not doing it right. Another participant explained this very well:

> I had a breakthrough in all of this kind of thing a couple of years ago when I realised that it's the nature of any clairvoyant experience for us to all see it differently. Then it all started working for me. This is how I explain it to myself:
>
> The "otherworld" where all this clairvoyant stuff happens is incomprehensible to our regular day-to-day minds, and so the part of us that lets us perceive it acts as a "translator" converting it into a language we can understand. So, for me, it might translate plant spirits into mythological creatures.; for you, into people; for others, into glowing beings of light.

My reply was that there is not a "correct" aura that would look the same to everyone. I see them rather like the Hodgson pictures, but a bit simpler—more like coloured flows of energy than fixed shapes, whereas the first participant quoted above described something more like classic fairy shapes.

So, to "see" them as humans is quite valid. What tells you that this clairvoyance is working is how those impressions begin to come more and more easily and readily. Look at a tree and, say, you get quite a strong impression of an old Indian man; another tree, and you see a different woman... If that is how it works for you, then your mind is using familiar human shapes to convey the information, whereas my mind tends to use colours and flows.

So, just keep seeing them that way until it becomes easy and feels spontaneous (the Cup mindset) and then you can start comparing. Do some types of trees seem female? Do others seem to be male? Is it younger trees that look like younger people? Do damaged trees look like wounded people? You may begin to notice some interesting patterns. One participant replied to this with:

> I think I'm starting to get the hang of this "playfulness" thing. I'm still doing this with trees and flowers, and it is slowly becoming a more spontaneous habit. Today I walked through a cemetery, and not only did I start seeing trees with human characteristics, but I also began to see "shapes", vague colours, and the odd abstract quality to each entity here and there.

> I think that some of my misgivings about this at the start came from the way I was projecting human characteristics onto something that was not human. For example, slender trees with pink flowers look "feminine". If a man had a slender figure and face, he is more likely to be seen as "effeminate", especially if he wears pink (the old-fashioned "blue for boys, pink for girls" thinking coming back into play). Large trees with thicker trunks and no flowers tend to look "masculine", just as a woman who is big-built and dresses like a tomboy is more likely to be regarded as "butch". I was afraid that all I was doing was walking through a park and saying to myself, "That tree looks a bit girly," or something.
>
> Now, I think that this kind of projection might be a start to something. Perhaps by allowing myself to do this, I stop censoring my imagination from allowing more information to come through.

"Allowing myself" was exactly the right expression. What the censor seems to do is pre-judge what we are allowed to see, and if one should get a glimpse of something "wrong", it will dismiss it as nothing, or as folly. At one level it is doing a useful job, maybe saving us from psychic or emotional overload, but at another it is making our decisions for us. So, rather than repress those projections, we observe them, and note if they are telling us something.

Once the material is coming through easily, by all means apply judgement to see if it is worthwhile. You might complete this course thinking, "I'm mostly choosing not to be clairvoyant because I don't find it very useful," but that is better than spending the rest of your life yearning: "I only wish I was clairvoyant".

CAN WE DO MORE THAN JUST LOOK AT THE FAIRIES?

Once you have got the knack of seeing devas, fairies, auras or whatever you choose to call them, then you can try to interact.

Approach a tree, see the spirit of the tree, then ask if you may enter the tree's shade or touch it—does the spirit respond?

Again, what happens is personal to you: maybe the spirit seems to speak back, maybe it gestures or maybe it changes colour or form. You are learning a whole new language.

Here's what another person experienced when they sent thoughts into the aura:

> I have a few new aquilegias in my kitchen window so I went to look at those and see what transpired. As I learned as a teenager that I can scry fog by slightly unfocussing my eyes and seeing the lights come towards me in pinpoints before the pictures form, I tried that with the young plants and immediately started getting lights moving

> around the leaves as described. Then I sent thoughts to one of them, that I wanted to see the spirit form, and it just sort of took shape from the movement. Very much like the paintings.
>
> I know a shrink would say I formed it with my imagination, as well as the feeling I got from it, but as one who has believed in nature spirits for most of my life, I have no doubt that something real was there. Whether imagination helps shape the perceived form is another matter.

HEALING THE WORLD THROUGH CLAIRVOYANCE

One participant described a previous experience of communicating with plants that shows how one can take this work further with practice:

> I love this stuff. As far as I am concerned this communication with these nature intelligences is the most important work. A few years ago when I first started experimenting with communicating with nature, inspired by the work at Findhorn and Perelandra, I was told about a village that was having big problems with their pond. Somebody had introduced a very pretty but invasive New Zealand pond weed which was totally dominating and suffocating all the other pond life. I felt that I could do something about this so I contacted the local wildlife trust for permission to work with the

pond. I took some photos and collected a sample of the weed.

My understanding was that all that humans create can be considered as gardens. Nature does not do gardens; they are our speciality. So in this case the little plant, after being dumped in the pond, thrived. It thought: "I have been put here. There are no predators, so let's go for it!"

Back at my desk I montaged the photos together and then asked to be connected to the plant. The experience blew me away—the feeling of sweetness and of surprise at communication. The Deva was confused: "I have been put in the pond and now I am being cursed and ripped out of the water and I can feel that I am not wanted..."

I explained to the plant that it was welcome but needed to chill out—just don't be so rampant, be in balance with every thing else in the ecosystem.

It worked. The pond returned to balance and has stayed that way for a few years. It probably needs another session, because a different plant is now dominating.

SEEING AURAS, A FINAL STEP

Last week I revealed my simple trick that allowed me to "see" nature spirits, devas and auras. If it "worked" for you—in the sense that you now have a taste of something that you previously thought you were blind to—then I invite you to continue practising it this week.

What initially might have been just an effort of imagination—"I guess I should see a little grey gnome with a blue hat, that's nice"—can soon gather momentum and become increasingly spontaneous and even surprising: "That's interesting, I feel sure that one should be blue while this one just *has* to be green and wispy. I wonder why?"

Gazing at a bed of daffodils is always a pleasure, but now you can gaze longer, and in a different way, seeing other forms of life emerging with surprising and increasing vividness. It becomes interesting, it adds value, yet for me it remains an effort and is never totally spontaneous. I think that is how it is meant to be for me: an additional item in my magical toolkit, rather than a natural, ongoing ability.

So this week I suggest some ways to extend that exercise, and then add one further exercise.

Exercise 1—Further Work With Nature Spirits

This is just an extension of the flower fairy exercise. Having got used to doing it—to the point where you can glance at any plant and quickly form an impression of what its deva or aura looks like—now see if you can communicate with it.

For a start, look for signs in the vision of the plant's well-being. When I was running Week Five of the Arcanorium course, I went to a local bonsai exhibition—a wonderful opportunity to look at the auras of trees close-up and in miniature, and see all the variations in shape and colour. There I noticed one bonsai appeared to have a very weak and sickly aura compared with the others. Then I read the label, and saw that it was featured in the exhibition as a demonstration of a sick bonsai, with hints on how to recognise it was suffering.

This is one useful extension of the exercise: exploring a plant's health by looking for changes in the deva vision. Remember last week how one participant studied the gnomes in the rocks beside the road and commented: "Very sad they looked, unhappy at being blasted out of a cliff, and straining to get back into the earth, where they belong."

When we buy a plant for the garden, the question often arises as to where it should be planted, to look good but also as to where it will best flourish. Try experimenting with this method: take the plant in its pot, observe its deva, and then place it in different likely positions to see how its deva reacts. If one position seems to make the deva extra happy, perhaps that is where it should be planted. Does the deva, in your case, react quickly to a situation, or does it need to be left there for a few hours to have time to assess the spot?

CAN WE ACTUALLY CONVERSE WITH PLANTS AND ROCKS?

Remember also that another participant described a conversation with the imported pondweed—hearing how puzzled the plant was at being hated, but also explaining to the plant why its alien invasion was a problem.

Can you converse with a plant? Well, you can certainly talk to them, whether they listen or not. Charles, Prince of Wales, is often mocked by the media as someone who talks to his plants (the fact that some of those media critics earn their living by talking to a camera is seldom mentioned). There are plenty of good reasons why one can benefit from treating plants and other objects as if they were sentient beings, as explained in *Uncle*

Ramsey's Little Book of Demons (2005), and so talking to plants becomes one of those things that proves highly sensible, though not very reasonable (in the terminology of my introduction to this book).

It is, however, a big step from simply talking to a plant or rock to getting an intelligible answer in return. We took the first step above when we started looking for signs of happiness or illness in a deva—essentially a way of reading the answer to the question, "How are you feeling?" But the conversation with the invasive pondweed clearly went way beyond that.

So let us say that, instead of moving the plant to different potential planting spots and watching for its reaction, we simply stood before the plant and asked, "Where would you like to be planted?" What sort of answer might we expect?

The answer depends firstly on how you see the plant's spirit. If it appears as a semi-human form, like a fairy or gnome, then you might hope for a spoken or sign-language answer to come from it. But if it appears as a wispy aura, as in the Hodson pictures, then it is more likely to communicate in flows of movement and colour—the aura might reach out in a particular direction, or point high or low, or maybe change colour in a suggestive way.

Very few people get a clear spoken answer that seems to come from the plant. What is much more likely is that an answer simply flashes into your mind as if by telepathy. This brings us back to the same problem that stops people from seeing fairies in the first place. As I said last week, if you allow fantasy to help you see fairies as I suggest, you have to work against the left brain complaining that, "This isn't clairvoyance, it's just fantasy". The same applies here: when you ask the plant where it wants to be planted, and the words "in the shade by the pool" jump into your mind, then the rational faculty will tend to analyse and insist that it was just your mind working out the answer, not the plant.

The solution, as before, is simply to remain in the Cup (right-brain) state and accept that answer. Allow it to happen and go on practising until these answers come easier and easier. Go up to an ancient oak tree and ask it what Autumn feels like, how it feels about pigs eating its acorns, or about people using it for timber. Gaze at a beautiful landscape and ask it if it enjoys being looked at, about how it feels when houses are built on it or a road passes through. Keep working at this and make a note of the answers you get.

Then, what about the left-brain question? Is it all just your own brain thinking up these answers? That is for you to decide. In my case I have had enough interesting and surprising answers to conclude that, even if the form of wording was mediated through my brain, the content of the answers was interesting enough to justify taking it at face value.

In Winchester, I once stood in a nature reserve and felt unhappy that this beautiful and serene place was spoiled by the roar of traffic on a main road just beyond the trees. So I asked the deva of the place how it coped with this intrusion. The answer was that, while the deva could see I was offended by the noise, Nature herself had for millions of years lived with roaring lions, crashing dinosaurs, lightning and rockfalls, so that the noise was nothing. I then asked the deva why my pendulum had led me to two distinct "creative centres" in Winchester (I was at the time doing the dowsing exercise described in Week 3). The reply was that a man has only one creative matrix, his brain, whereas a woman has two, her brain and her womb.

In Gloucestershire I was asked to collect poles to make a sweat lodge and so felt I was really getting into the cosmic spirit of the event by asking a willow tree in high-flown language if I might invite it to share our experience by offering some branches for the lodge. The reply was, "Cut that New Age crap. You just want to lop bits off me like everyone else does. But thanks for asking, and help yourself."

So, as with seeing nature spirits, the right approach to conversing with them is to simply practise until it comes easily, then decide if it is worth doing, and only then, if you really need to, start analysing what is happening and where it comes from.

Exercise 2—Seeing Auras

If you have by now learnt how to see the spirit (or aura) of a plant, then the next step is to ask whether you can see a person's aura by the same means. The answer is yes, but I've found there are complications.

Begin in the same way as with a plant. Gaze at someone and ask yourself what you would expect their aura to look like. Again, as with the story-telling tarot, rather than doing it for a known person as a "reading", choose a stranger in a crowd, or waiting at the supermarket checkout, so the aura reading is simply a game and does not initially carry the burden of having to be true, or meaningful, or a deduction from what you already know about the person.

I never got far with his myself—and the auras I saw tended to be diverse shapes more than the traditional sheath around the body—but the reason I stopped is interesting in itself. What I found was that, when I gazed at a person in this way, they tended to turn around and stare back at me. Embarrassing, but also interesting because it suggests that my "aura reading" trick was something more than just an individual exercise of the imagination. There seemed to be some sort of information exchange that often the subject could also sense.

That is good, because it suggests that the exercise of seeing devas is more than just a fantasy taking root in my mind, it is some sort of actual exchange of information with the object. It is a proper communication. (You see, I am still in dialogue with the Dagger in my mind, convincing it to allow added value into my life.)

Having stopped trying this, it left me with only one interesting experience to relate. One time, I looked at the auras of a man and a woman walking purposefully down the street ahead of me. They were not walking as a couple, but as two busy, independent people. Then I noticed a white tentacle emerge from the man's aura towards the woman and curl round her. Less than five seconds later he reached his arm round her waist and they walked on.

COMMENTS ON EXERCISE 2

One participant said he'd been trying for years to see auras and, like myself, he usually received shapes rather than colours. But he too found that if he stopped trying to "see" the aura and just allowed information to come, then he began getting good results. The course he described as "a massive confidence booster—mostly because I've realised that, in fact, I *can* do this stuff, I just don't acknowledge it." If you, the reader of this book, obtain the same benefit I will be delighted.

One of the many filters presented by the left-brain "Dagger" mind is the sense of disappointment—"A deva should have lovely colours, and all I see is a human figure"; "Auras should look like a sheaf of colours, and all I see is a shape"; "Surely the pendulum ought to lead me in the right direction even when I'm trying to make it go the other way," and so on. An expectation is not lived up to, and so the information received is dismissed and forgotten with the thought: "I'm obviously not psychic".

But if we accept that a non-verbal right-brain part of our mind is trying to communicate something to us, then we should simply note *any* data arriving in our minds and be prepared to interpret it as if learning a totally new language.

In trying to express this, I emphasised the importance of delaying the analysis function. If, when first trying to see a flower deva all you see is a little man, then the next thing to do is let that happen many times to confirm whether this is a consistent reaction. Once it begins to look reliable, you can then start noting the variations and look for patterns that might reveal some form of language: Do big plants go with big people? Do plants from other continents go with people looking like natives of those continents? Do the healthiest plants produce the healthiest looking people?

Any of these things are reasonable questions to ask, yet they might also prove quite wrong. As when interpreting the message of a dream symbol, whatever you experience is a personal message to you, but in an unknown language. When I looked at that sick bonsai, I "saw" the flow of colour as shrunken and with little activity; but another person might have seen the sickness symbolised as a goblin on a stretcher; another might just have seen a fragment of surgical dressing or a crashed car as their symbol of ill-health.

Another participant found, when trying to see a person's aura, neither colour nor shape but a strong feeling of compassion for the person they were looking at. That was on her first attempt, but when she went into town she found:

> Lots of people are repellent. Others leave snail-like trails behind them. Yuk! I should

> add that others were lovely and colourful, and yet others were dull or had nothing at all.

Another person found:

> I practised the Week 6 exercises and the shapes I see around people seem to be dependent on their posture somehow—like some kind of electromagnetic field around their body. Only occasionally I get the impression of a colour. It's mostly vague forms.
>
> The most dramatic experience I had this week was in work. I tried reading a person's aura, after some practice, and I got a kind of "demonic" look from him. I thought that was interesting, as all I ever got with other people, if anything, was vague shapes around this body, often around their heads. Sometimes I don't even see anything, but sense a general personality trait to them (which I often still suspect is purely down to me reading their body language).

Suggestions for Further Work

First, I remind you of the importance of that "total awareness" walking exercise in the first week, and how it can be seen as a fundamental practice to strengthen right-brain consciousness. Practise that and you will regain the sense of newness and surprise in everyday life, for this is how the brain handles first impressions. "Become as a little child," but preferably seen and not heard.

I won't recommend specific books on further psychic practice, because most bookshops seem to be full of such texts under the heading "Mind Body Spirit," or the like. So simply choose the ones that interest you.

Reading some of these books you might find yourself thinking, "What planet does this guy come from?" The answer to that question is not to worry about the guy's planet but to read his instructions in the same playful Cup spirit that this course should have engendered. However dogmatic the book's writer might seem, don't be put off as long as the exercises work. The principles given in these past six weeks will go a long way to helping you develop many other psychic powers. Here are a few examples.

OTHER FORMS OF DIVINATION

Crystal-gazing is a difficult one for me, because the act of staring at a particular crystal tends to focus my attention in a Dagger-like manner rather than open me up in the Cup-like receptive spirit. So the only success I have had with crystal-gazing has been when I stop trying to do it "by the book" and instead just hold a crystal with my eyes half or fully closed and then take a sort of day-dream walk into it. So I am not so much looking into the crystal for a vision, as allowing it to lead me on an inner journey—more like the process of getting a deva to speak to you in Week 6.

Systems of divination like the I Ching, where one looks up the interpretation in a book, are interesting because the book is words and so is essentially giving you a left-brain message. Sometimes the words are so literally correct that a meaning just leaps out from the page—bearing in mind that the process may be selective, i.e. one particular sentence provides all the meaning you need and the rest is largely ignorable. More generally, I read the interpretation through once or twice and then let the mind hold this input in the Cup-like state and allow messages to float up to the surface.

As an example of this: once my life was unhappily riven because I was wooing a maiden in London and that required me every weekend to leave my home in Gloucestershire and drive up to the city—and I was feeling rootless and torn between the two locations. The I Ching reading was something about a king travelling all over his domain—but I did not feel at all like a king, more like an unwilling messenger boy. Then I realised that I had been seeing my trips to London as an enforced wrenching away from my domain in the Cotswolds, whereas I could choose to see all of Britain (or the world) as my domain. In that spirit, the journeys could feel more like a king visiting the outposts of his kingdom. That realisation provided the just the sort of healing I had looked for when I first asked the I Ching the question.

Despite what I said about the story-telling exercise, I myself tend to read tarot in that same literary way, using the Crowley/Harris pack and reading the interpretations in one or more of the good books on that tarot. It was, however, the story-telling exercise that first got me into reading tarot.

Very different forms of divination are those such as reading tea leaves, where instead of stock symbols or written phrases the diviner receives abstract shapes that he or she has to read sense into. Like looking at clouds, you might think a particular leaf looks a bit like a camel, while another person might see it as an laden table. Don't worry what others think, just let your mind make up stories in the spirit of the tarot game and you'll not go wrong.

The ultimate version of such open-ended divination is to simply walk out into the world with a question in mind. When the diviner has an important question, rather than throwing bones, or tarots or whatever, one just walks in nature "looking for a sign". Something (anything) happens that feels significant, and then the mind ponders that happening to interpret the symbol as an answer to the question.

"What should I do about my current health problems?" As you walk away from the house you find you are suddenly intensely aware of the spring flowers that you had not noticed before—is that saying, "Time to make a new start"? Or the neighbour's dog that usually barks at you seems much more friendly today—is it a message to be more sociable? Or that you need a companion to cheer you up? No matter what the actual occurrence, it is the sense of significance that attracts your attention and then, just as if it were a dream symbol, you look for possible messages and follow the interpretation that feels most significant and seems most to come to life. As you pat the dog and ponder your social life, your heart sinks. Then you wonder what it would feel like to walk out with a close companion and you feel a surge of happiness... That is the way to go, so explore further.

CHANNELING OR AUTOMATIC WRITING

This is another example where we are looking for a particular form of co-operation between the two main brain functions. Channelling and automatic writing involve receiving messages in a written language, and that is the domain of the left brain, and yet the material comes more from the right brain.

The process is most akin to that communication with a deva, looking for words that spring into your mind. For most people they are words that appear as telepathic thoughts, raising the same question, "Isn't this just my own thoughts?" I suggest the same answer: allow these thoughts to arise, collect them, then judge them by their merit.

Reading other people's channelled writing, I am aware that a lot of it is junk. Maybe the wording is padded out with quaintisms, such as: "I give thee my word, oh Seeker on the Path, that the Mighty Ones of the Cosmos do justly aver that—blah blah..." For the sceptical right brain that sort of wording is enough to label the whole process as rubbish, but that is like reaching into a goldmine, pulling out a handful of dirt and so deciding to abandon the mine. Judge what you receive not by the worst bits, but by the best bits. (But by all means judge what *others* receive by the worst bits—it's a good laugh and you can hardly blame the left brain for enjoying it.)

Automatic writing is a little more dramatic: you allow the hand holding the pen to scribble as it chooses. A planchette (or "Ouija") board can help, but this is far more effective when a group uses it.

One practice that lies between the two is the sort of automatic writing practised by the Surrealists before the war. Basically, you take a pad of paper and a pencil and start writing off the top of your head as fast as you can, anything that comes into your mind without any care for punctuation or spelling or grammar. After a while you simply tire out and your mind goes blank. You then force the pace by using a stock phrase—something like, "And another consideration is..." just to keep yourself from stopping. You may well find you are simply covering a whole sheet of paper with one phrase, or one word over and over. Eventually such an exercise leads to a wonderful silencing of the mind, which is just exhausted by expressing itself. The state is not unlike the total awareness exercise of Week 1.

What do you do in that state? You can just hold it like a meditation, or you can use it as a starting point for right-brain communication—start writing slowly words that come into your mind. If you invite those words to be channelled from a higher authority, then they may take on a special quality. They will be channelled words.

Automatic drawing is a similar process, an extension of the mindless doodling that takes place when the mind is otherwise distracted, but it bypasses the left-brain linguistic channel because it uses images and movement instead of words and language.

HEALING

A lot of the exercises in this book have healing potential. I have explained above how an I Ching reading helped heal a concern of mine. A tarot reading could do the same. More than one participant realised that my body awareness exercise in Week 2 held the key to better health through eating right, as well as vetting potential remedies by dowsing.

One participant had used something like the aura exercise to locate other people's bodily abnormalities:

> When I was a university student, it was general knowledge that I was into "weird stuff" and, to play to the crowd, I learned a few party-pieces. A "trick" that used to keep me in free beer for some time was finding old broken bones or injuries. I used to slowly move my hand, about three or four inches away, over the person, with a little "energy ball" in my hand when I did it.

Almost without fail, if I passed it over the site of a previous serious injury, I got a hot, almost electric sensation—as did the person.

Finding a hidden problem like this can be a first diagnostic stage to healing. If, for example, someone has persistent headaches, you might locate the cause to be a tension in the spine, or an old wound to the neck. Moving on to active healing of the problem could be like communicating with a deva, as explained in Week 6. If the person has persistent stomach pains, you could "ask" the stomach what the problem is and listen for an answer.

I won't elaborate on this, because it is a very big topic and there are probably many specialist books on psychic healing to guide you. The main message for now is that books on topics like healing tend to plug a particular terminology or party line—the subject has been formalised into a named "discipline" in order to appease the left-brain bias in our society. By all means follow that party line but, if it begins to obscure the healing process, just remember the basic exercises and principles in this book and they will help you navigate through the mumbo jumbo.

ANIMAL COMMUNICATION

I said a bit in Week 6 about talking to plants. Surely talking to animals is a more obvious choice?

Basically, the principle is the same. When you ask a question, you don't expect the cat or creature to look at you and vocalise a reply in perfect, clipped BBC English. Instead you look for some sign of comprehension or recognition as you would look for it in the plant's deva.

Does that look actually convey an answer? For example: if you ask a dog whether it wants to go for a walk and it not only looks you straight in the eye, as if acknowledging your question, but also wags its tail and squeals with every sign of joy—then the answer is a resounding "yes".

In many cases the answer needs more than body language or gesture. If you want to know how a cat feels about you going away on holiday for a fortnight, you want more than a straight miaow. Here you can practise something more like conversing with a deva: look at the cat and calmly put your question to it, aloud or in your head, and listen for an answer as you would to a plant deva. The answer should just pop into your head as you gaze at the cat. As with the deva, the trick is not to let the Dagger stop this happening, but to let an answer come and then, instead of analysing where the answer came from (e.g. "I bet it was just wishful thinking on my part") you should use your analytical power to see if it was a good answer.

So, let us say you get the reply: "I'm okay with you being away as long as the shed window is left securely open so I can always get in there and someone checks the food and water every other day." Take that answer then meditate on it. Does it feel really good? Picture the shed window held properly open and the cat being adequately fed, does that feel right? Do you now feel at ease about your question? Then you can trust the answer, even though it did not apparently come out of the cat's mouth.

This is the basic approach to animal communication. If you believe it is possible, then you can be less invasive. Instead of reaching to grab a strange cat in order to pet it—because that is the only way you know how to communicate with cats—just sit in its presence and do not stare. Instead let your positive feelings flow towards it and inwardly invite it to respond. If it begins to show an interest, take that as encouragement and mentally speak to it in a friendly way. And so on.

Again, specialist books will take you further in this, but the basic principles have been covered in these six weeks.

PREDICTING THE FUTURE

For some people, this is what psychic powers are all about. It's a good example of what I said right at the beginning, about making the subject of psychism weird in order to keep it away.

The argument goes a bit like this: "Oh, so you claim to be psychic do you? Okay then, tell me who's going to win the Grand National next week, or what the FTSE100 share index will be in one week's time. Can't do it? Well, you're not much of a psychic are you!"

Big banks hire highly-trained people and use vastly expensive computer systems trying to predict next week's share prices and, when they often get it wrong, they don't rubbish the computer and sack the staff, they just try harder next time. And yet the sceptic pretends to be amazed that an amateur with a few psychic powers cannot do the same job off the top of his head. They insist on making such extreme claims for psychism that they have launched it into the outer space of impossibility.

My own experience of using psychic powers to predict the future is that they are not very good at it. Clairvoyance in its many forms can be amazingly accurate at detecting where someone is and where they are going on their life's path, but so many unexpected things can happen to deflect you from that path.

For example, you might go to a tarot reader and ask for a reading without telling them much about yourself and be told that—let us say—"You are very upset about your family circumstances at present, but in actual fact the real problem is uncertainty about your choice of career, and whether you should change before it's too late".

Sometimes a reading like that can hit the nail on the head so accurately as to make you gasp: in a few words it has got to the bottom of your anxiety in a way that makes it abundantly clear where the solution lies. That is the real value of most readings. If, however, the reader goes on to say: "You will change your job later this year, but it is only in five years time that you really find your true path," that is also interesting, and helpful as a positive suggestion, but often such predictions don't work out much better than predictions by economists, scientists, politicians or other highly-paid experts.

If you have developed your psychic powers as described in this course, you will not only be better at predicting the future, you will also have a healthy scepticism about unreasonable expectations for predicting the future by any means, psychic or otherwise. I'm tempted to say, "Keep it to yourself".

MAKING THINGS HAPPEN

This is even worse than predicting the future: "Okay, if you've got psychic powers, prove it by turning this heap of shit into a gold ingot for me!"

Forget it.

Some amazing things happen when you start exercising psychic powers, but the real value lies in making life richer and more interesting. Whereas a universe that can be controlled would soon become boring.

The analogy I often give is this: you see waves beating on a shore and someone asks you if you can control the waves and make them rise and fall at your command. The answer is no, you have no control over the waves. Doesn't that mean you are completely at the mercy of life's waves? Along comes a surfer: he has absolutely no power to force the waves to do his bidding, and yet he can flow with those waves and perform miracles before your very eyes.

Don't fight it, *feel* it. Go with the flow, and you will still obtain a lot of what you aspire to.

Conclusion

The premise of this course is that—rather than assume some people are psychic and others not—we assume that we all receive more information than is necessary, and that our brains have learnt to screen out a lot of it. This filtering has become so automatic that many in Western society are convinced that they cannot or should not receive psychic data, and can no longer choose to remove or reduce the filters.

So we began by stretching the familiar: how you listen to music must make some difference to the way it sounds, so let's see if we can tell the difference. We then explored ways to increase sensory awareness by being as receptive as a Cup and learning to delay the critical Dagger filters until something worthwhile had been perceived—at which point we may by all means examine the results critically and see if they were truly worthwhile—i.e. did opening myself to this particular psychic data really add value to my existence?

Then a series of exercises explored ways to become more sensitive to:

1. location and situation;
2. our body's responses and needs;
3. the underlying spirit of a town or region;

4. the symbols of a tarot pack and our own chosen life symbols;

5. winning boardgame strategies;

6. and the auras or spirits of nature.

Each exercise had its own place and value within this course as a way to practise the open, Cup-like frame of mind and allow it freedom to play without being too rapidly censored by the critical Dagger part of the mind.

But most of the exercises could also have value in themselves. For example, the ability to listen to my body's needs has been important to me and my health for many years, and has become a regular habit. Increased sensory awareness has also been useful at times.

So, I invite you to use your critical Dagger faculties to think over these exercises and how they went for you, in order to decide not so much whether they were "real" or "proved" you are psychic, but rather whether one or more of them might add value to your experience. Then you can decide whether to add those to your magical toolkit, or even make them part of your life.

You can leave this book behind you like a chance encounter, an interesting experience, or you can develop a relationship with some part of it and let it become part of your life.

A new openness to Nature. A revitalised sense of space and surroundings. A fuller enjoyment of pictorial symbols. What was just a tree now becomes a friend. Washing cars becomes a meditation. Or whatever...

May you, the reader, make even better use of these powers than I have.

Notes

1. One of the best resources on pendulums that I've found is by Tom Graves, at: http://tinyurl.com/3xq9rz3 (tomgraves.org).

2. At the time of writing, *Elements of Pendulum Dowsing* by Tom Graves can be downloaded from: http://tinyurl.com/2uvh43v (tetradianbooks.com).

3. At the time of writing, *A Letter to Robin* by Walt Woods is available from: http://tinyurl.com/374f9pn (lettertorobin.org).

4. At the time of writing, the paper can be download from: http://tinyurl.com/347opym (angelfire.com).

5. The William Gray tarot can be viewed at: http://tinyurl.com/3xj3a3g (lelandra.com).

6. To give an idea of the very many tarots you could choose from, one student suggested this amazing website: http://tinyurl.com/ylz6ddc (aeclectic.net).

References

Ramsey Dukes (1979). *Thundersqueak.* The Mouse That Spins.

Ramsey Dukes (2003). *BLAST Your Way to Megabuck$ with my SECRET Sex-Power Formula.* The Mouse That Spins.

Ramsey Dukes (2005). *Uncle Ramsey's Little Book of Demons.* London: Aeon.

Tom Graves (1986). *The Diviner's Handbook.* Rochester, VT: Destiny Books.

Tom Graves (2008). *Elements of Pendulum Dowsing.* Tetradian Books.

Geoffrey Hodson (1952). *The Kingdom of the Gods.* Theosophical Publishing House.

Walt Woods (2001). *A Letter to Robin.* http://www.lettertorobin.org.